COVER MAGIC

Edited by

DOROTHEA HALL

~

Loose covers created by

RON CAROLISSEN

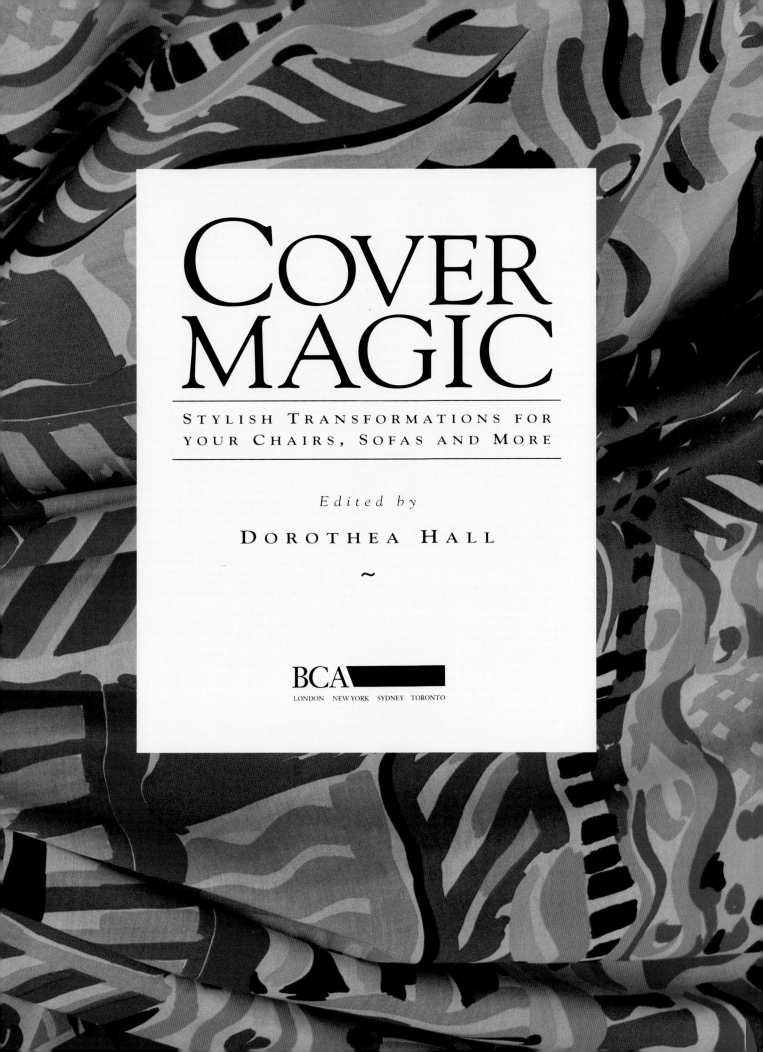

COVER MAGIC

STYLISH TRANSFORMATIONS FOR YOUR CHAIRS, SOFAS AND MORE

Edited by

DOROTHEA HALL

~

BCA

LONDON NEW YORK SYDNEY TORONTO

This edition published 1995 by BCA
by arrangement with
Cassell plc, Villiers House,
41–47 Strand,
London WC2N 5JE

Copyright © 1995 Quarto Publishing plc

All rights reserved. No part of this
publication may be reproduced in any
material form (including photocopying or
storing it in any medium by electronic
means and whether or not transiently or
incidentally to some other use of this
publication) without the written
permission of the copyright owner, except
in accordance with the provisions of the
Copyright, Designs and Patents Act 1988
or under the terms of a licence issued by
the Copyright Licensing Agency, 90
Tottenham Court Road, London W1P
9HE. Applications for the copyright
owner's written permission to reproduce
any part of this publication should be
addressed to the publisher.

This book was designed and produced by
Quarto Publishing plc
The Old Brewery
6 Blundell Street
London N7 9BH

Editor Laura Washburn
Art Editor Julie Francis
Designer Debbie Mole
Illustrator Elsa Godfrey
Photographer Paul Forrester
Picture Researchers Jo Carlill,
Susannah Jayes
Art Director Moira Clinch
Editorial Director Sophie Collins

CN 4732

Typeset in Great Britain by
Genesis Typesetting, Rochester
Manufactured by
Regent Publishing Services Ltd,
Hong Kong
Printed by
Leefung Asco Printers Ltd, China

CONTENTS

FABRIC FACTS

DON'T GET completely carried away by a fabric's design before you have also considered its suitability for the job you intend it to do. First check what it is made of, how well it will wear, how easy it will be to clean and if it is safe to use.

Furnishing fabric fibres

Furnishing fabrics are made from a wide range of fibres that fall into two main categories.

Natural fibres Wool, linen, cotton and silk are resistant to dirt and clean well. However they can shrink when washed and cotton, linen and silk may crease.

Man-made fibres There are two types of man-made fibres: those derived from natural materials but treated with chemicals and those that are totally synthetic. Rayon and viscose are made from regenerated plant material which has been chemically treated. They are unlikely to shrink, but are less resistant to wear than synthetics.

Synthetic fibres Acrylic, nylon and polyester, amongst others, are usually stronger than natural fibres. They are crease resistant, mothproof and usually shrink proof. However the fibres attract dirt and so a synthetic fabric needs more frequent washing. Many fabrics are made up of a mix of natural and man-made fibres so that the benefits of each may be combined.

Think about the suitability of fabric for the task at hand.

Fabric options

Choose a tough, hard wearing fabric that is closely woven for loose covers as they take a lot of hard wear. Linen union, a mixture of linen and cotton, is the traditional choice but medium weight cotton, ticking or a tough cotton and polyester mix are all suitable. Avoid very thick fabrics as these are difficult to sew, especially if you include piping in the seams. Large designs can look very effective but bear in mind they take accurate positioning and there is likely to be a lot of wastage when you centre the design. Also think about aftercare of your fabric. Machine washable fabrics are easier to live with but you will be limited in your choice as most furnishing fabrics require dry cleaning.

Shopping for fabric

Before you buy fabric check that it has no flaws and that the design has been printed on to it straight. As you need to cut lengths across the grain accurately a design that is askew can cause real problems. Buy too much

Fabric can be indoors or outdoors, practical or whimsical.

There are many factors to consider when choosing your fabric. Consider the use of your cover: will it be indoors or outdoors, or both, and will it need to be changed with the seasons. The fabric on this chair is a good example of a practical, all-around choice.

rather than too little fabric as it is important it all comes from the same batch number. This means that it has been printed at the same time so the colour will be the same throughout. A later batch can come up slightly different. Some cheap fabrics may have been bulked out with dressing to look of better quality than they really are. When washed the dressing disappears to leave a thin, limp material. Rub the fabric to check for dressing.

Hall chairs, or other items that are ornamental, can be covered in any fabric, even lace, and the effect is stunning.

QUESTIONS TO ASK BEFORE YOU BUY FABRIC

1 Will it wear well?
Loose covers and chair seat cushions take a lot of wear and need to be made from tough fabrics if they are to last.

2 Will it clean easily?
Check that washable fabrics will not shrink or wash before you use them but be aware that they may continue to shrink to some degree. Cushion covers will probably need more regular cleaning. Loose covers and upholstery fabrics gain from having a stain resistant finish. Some fabrics have already been treated or treatment may be available.

3 Will it look good?
Fabrics used for gathered or pleated furnishings need to drape well. Check this before buying. Check that sofa and cushion cover fabrics will not crease. Crumple them in your hand then watch to see if the creases quickly disappear when you release them.

4 Is it safe to use?
It is important to use flame-resistant fabrics on sofas and chairs. Look for the label or ask in the shop.

5 Will it be exposed to bright light?
Strong sunlight fades fabrics quickly, especially is you choose bright colours. Look for fade-proof fabrics.

6 What style do I want to create?
The elements of a room will look most effective if they have style as a unifying factor. Pick a style you like; country cottage, farmhouse, formal, period, minimal or whatever then keep fabrics, flooring, furniture and wall decoration to the same theme.

Let fabric work for you to create rooms that are both beautiful and comfortable.

CREATING WITH COLOUR

COLOUR IS the most obvious and exciting element in a room and for this reason it is easy to be fearful of making a mistake when creating a colour scheme. However it is not difficult to put colours together that complement and enhance each other, and the room where they appear, if you follow a few simple ground rules. The most interesting homes are those that highlight the characters of the inhabitants, so start by collecting samples of colour combinations that please you.

Combine neutral tones with fabric pattern and texture.

Absence of colour can also be an effective basis for an interior decor scheme and loose covers, which can be removed for easy washing, are ideal for a white fabric.

Using neutrals

Apart from true colours, dealt with in the colour wheel, there are the neutrals, those shades which contain no colour. These are black, white and grey. Beige and all its tones – cream, mushroom, off-white, fawn, stone, sand, tan and so on – are usually referred to as neutrals too. A neutral is often used as the basis for a restrained scheme, then small splashes of colour are added to provide interest. Neutrals can also be used together very effectively to create a rustic, natural look. This is most successful where a wide range of textures is also included.

The colour wheel shows how colours work together and against each other to achieve the desired effect.

Contrast colours are those that work best together.

Putting colours together

It is easiest to work with colour if you start by using a colour wheel. The colour wheel, like a rainbow, is made up of red, orange, yellow, green, blue and violet. Each of these colours is interspersed by the colour which is a mixture of the two on either side of it. Using tones of one colour, known as a monochromatic scheme, can be very effective, but choose the tones carefully. A yellow green will not look good beside a blue green. To ensure success pick tones from the same side of the true colour. So mix blue greens only with other blue greens or yellow-greens with other yellow-greens. Closely related colours, that is colours which lie next to each other on the colour wheel, are considered harmonious when used together and provide a background that is easy to live with. A harmonious colour scheme could include sand and terracotta, or lavender and pink, or denim blue and aqua. However a scheme made up totally of tones of one colour or of harmonious colours can be bland. Contrasting colours (known in the trade confusingly as complementary) lie on the opposite side of the colour wheel and a contrast colour can be used very effectively to enhance the main colour. The contrast is best used in small amounts as colour accents. Imagine a green sofa piped in red or aqua cushions displayed on an apricot covered chair. Look at fabric designs and you will see how often a small amount of a contrast colour has been introduced and how well this accent colour shows off the main shades and lifts the whole design.

Blue adds a cool tone as well as a restful atmosphere to rooms in which it is used.

Hot and cold colours affect our feelings about a fabric.

Hot and cold colours

By looking at the colour wheel you can also see that colours fall into one of two categories, warm or cool. Those on one side of the wheel, red, orange and yellow, are warm colours while those on the opposite side – green, blue and violet – are cool colours. This allows you to create a feeling of warmth in a sunless north-facing room by using a warm colour or, alternatively, to provide a cool atmosphere by using blue, green or violet tones in sunny south-facing rooms where you want to create a restful effect. Remember, too, that warm colours are stimulating whereas cool colours are relaxing.

Effect of colour on space

Cool colours appear to recede from you, warm colours to come towards you. Therefore a room decorated in cool colours will appear more spacious than one decorated in warm colours, which will look more cosy. However the strength of colour you use will also have an effect on this feeling of space. Light tones, or tints in which a little colour has been added to white, will also make a room appear spacious. A room's dimensions can be changed visually by clever use of colour in other ways. A high ceiling will appear lower if it is painted in a deeper tone of the wall colour. A light-coloured floor covering will also make a room appear larger, as will low furniture that matches the floor covering in colour. A picture rail or dado rail painted in a dark colour will diminish the sense of space in a room. Make a hall, or long, narrow room appear shorter by painting side walls and doors in a light tone, end walls and doors in a deeper tone.

Yellow warms up a room and adds a lively note to the decor.

Successful colour matching

Few people are able to carry colours accurately in their minds. It is much wiser to take samples of chosen paint colours, fabric swatches and furniture tones with you when you go to choose other items for a room. If you do not have a sample then match the colour up to a length of embroidery silk or a reel of sewing thread and take this instead. Always bring home samples of alternative choices before you buy. Pin all the samples – fabric, paint, wallcovering, carpet and so on – to a board and leave this in the room where the scheme is to be used for a few days. View the samples in both day and artificial light. This is important as lighting changes colours dramatically.

CHOOSING COLOURS – SEVEN POINTS TO BEAR IN MIND

1 Where do I start?
Few people have the chance to decorate a room from scratch. Consider all the points below if you have this opportunity. Otherwise consider existing colours or patterns when choosing additions.

2 Which exposure?
Bring sun to a north facing room with warm colours: yellow, apricot, red or pink. In a sunny south-facing room where you want a cool, sophisticated effect go for blue, lilac or green.

3 Do I want the room to appear larger or more cosy?
Cool colours or pale tones used on all the surfaces will make the room appear more spacious. Warm colours will provide a cosy look, strong shades will create a dramatic effect.

4 Is the area used over long periods or just passed through?
Frequently used rooms are generally best decorated in pale, easy to live with and restful tones. Use more exciting and brighter colour schemes for halls, landings, bathrooms or cloakrooms.

5 Is the room cluttered with furniture and accessories or simply furnished?
A room already 'busy' with bits and pieces looks best with a plain one-colour or neutral background. If you aim for a minimalist look a simply furnished room can also benefit if walls, flooring and furniture are kept to the same colour. Alternatively provide splashes of bright accent colour to give a simply furnished room interest.

6 Is it a room used mainly in the day or more at night?
Colours can look very different in daylight and artificial light so make sure you check your choice at the time when the room is in most constant use. In a brightly lit room the same colour will also appear less intense than in a dark room.

7 Can I be sure the colour I choose from a paint chart will look the same on the wall?
No! Because colours on a paint chart are usually surrounded by a border of white they appear paler than they really are. A good tip, if you have any doubts, is to go for the shade slightly lighter than the one you originally picked.

PATTERN AND TEXTURE

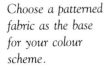

TOGETHER WITH colour, the choice of pattern and of texture are important elements in creating a room's character. Like colour they can make a room feel cosy or give it a spacious feeling.

The effects of pattern

Pattern creates an illusion of depth in a room. Small patterns appear to recede and therefore create a feeling of space in the same way that cool colours do. So use small patterns to make a small room larger. In a large room unless the design is very bold they pale into insignificance. Bold patterns, which like warm colours appear to come towards you, are best kept for large expanses of window, wall or floor and are ideal for loose covers, especially if the colour is strong. In a small space choose pale colours or they can easily be overpowering. If you want to use a large design in a small room consider using it in blinds with plain curtains at the window or wallpaper that goes up to dado height, then use plain paint or a textured paint finish above. Alternatively pick a bold design for matching loose covers and curtains then use plain toning colour for the walls and floorcovering. Pattern is a wonderful aid to changing a room's dimensions visually. Horizontal stripes will increase the apparent length of a wall, or use a picture or dado rail to create the effect. Vertical stripes will make a low ceiling appear higher. Widen a room with flooring in a pattern that runs across rather than along the room.

Placing a large motif in a central position on your cover makes for a stunning effect.

Choose a patterned fabric as the base for your colour scheme.

Planning with pattern

The simplest way to create a colour scheme is first to choose a fabric and then pick out colours from the design for plain walls and flooring, blinds and accessories. Re-introduce the pattern in small items like seat cushions, scatter cushions, lampshades or use it for piping.

Putting patterns together

The wide range of co-ordinated papers and fabrics provide many mix and match opportunities. To be sure of success use colour as the linking factor. If colour matches you can successfully mix geometric and floral patterns. For instance choose a bold floral fabric for curtains then pick out one of the colours from the fabric for striped wallpaper and the same colour to make loose covers from checked fabric.

Texture

Texture appeals to our sense of touch as well as sight. A surface may be rough or smooth, shiny or matt and these elements are tactile. They also work visually, like colour and pattern, to create space or to diminish it, to make a room appear cool or cosy. Shiny surfaces, such as satin and glazed fabrics for instance reflect light to create a feeling of space. But shiny surfaces are also cold-looking and too many can feel unfriendly. On the other hand textures that are rough, or soft with a matt finish such as wool, tweed and velvet, absorb light and provide a more cosy look. Although the effect is warm and comfortable, again, too much can also be claustrophobic. The most effective way to use texture is to mix shiny and matt, smooth and rough, hard and soft.

Use texture to add or diminish warmth in your interior.

Texture adds substance and drama to what could be an otherwise ordinary fabric.

GETTING THE MOST FROM PATTERNS AND TEXTURES

• Use pattern, like colour, to change the apparent shape of a room. To make a small room apear more spacious use mini-prints. Two-colour or two-tone paint effects also provide subtle pattern and texture.

• Texture changes colour, appearing much brighter on shiny surfaces, more muted or richer on matt surfaces. Use shiny surfaces to attract the eye to features you want to emphasize, and matt finishes to play down unattractive features.

• Tone down a too boldly patterned room with the introduction of sheer fabrics at the window or slatted blinds. These filter the light entering the room and soften colours.

• Extend the use of texture to the display of accessories. Break up the hard outline of a lamp base or picture with a feathery leaved plant.

BEFORE YOU BEGIN

Sewing your own loose cover is a truly rewarding experience, one which will give years of pleasure and fill you with pride, but there are certain steps that must be taken before you begin. This chapter covers the basics of loose cover making, from start to finish, and will help to clarify the fine points of loose cover sewing.

HOW TO USE THIS BOOK

Each project in this book begins with a Checklist. In this column you will find information to help you gather all the materials you need for the project, plus page references for specific techniques that are covered in-depth in the Techniques chapter. There is also an extensive explanation of how to measure your furniture, accompanied by a technical drawing.

The first illustration for each project is a **Cutting Layout**, which is a guideline for transposing the measurements obtained in Measuring Up into the squares and rectangles and sometimes shapes that will make up the pieces of the cover.

The **Techniques** section highlights basic sewing skills that are required for the project. Detailed information can be found in the various sections of the Techniques chapter.

The **Measuring Up** section tells you how to measure your furniture to calculate the amount of fabric needed.

FULL-LENGTH

This sophisticated cover was designed for a chair with a padded seat.

CHECKLIST

Materials

closely woven furnishing fabric
pre-shrunk piping cord
general sewing equipment   page 110–11

Techniques

piping and binding   page 118–19
frills and pleats   page 120–21

Measuring up

To the following measurements, add 1.5cm (⅝in) seam allowances:
Inside back – Measure the width plus the width of the struts and depth (A).
Outside back – Measure the width and depth to the seat (B).
Seat – Measure the width and depth (C).
Seat gusset – Measure the length from one back strut to the other and depth (D).
Skirt – Measure the depth and allow 1½ times the perimeter for the gather (E).
Ties – Allow eight pairs of ties, ours are 30 × 7cm (12 × 2¾in) (F).
Facings – Measure the width of the struts and the depth from top of chair to inside back seat edge (G).
Piping – Allow for bias strips (F).

▲ Using your measurements the cutting lines on the grain

▲ Make up enough piping f chair back, the gusset top and bottom and the top of the ba

▲ Place the inside back (A chair, wrong side out. Mark t seamlines. Pin a dart across t corners at right angles to the sides to accommodate the thi

▲ Right sides together, pin stitch the inside back to the (C); let the excess extend on side. Mark the seat seamline, front corners to fit, then trim

▲ Tack piping around the s front of the seat, right sides t extending to cover the fabric ance at each side of the insid

5 8

BEFORE YOU BEGIN
Be sure to read the following sections carefully. If it is your first time making a loose cover, it would be advisable to have a trial run through your chosen project using an inexpensive cotton fabric, such as curtain lining or calico. This is more time-consuming, but worth the effort if your chosen fabric is costly. In addition, if the trial cover fits perfectly, you can pick apart the seams and use the fabric sections as pattern pieces for your furnishing fabric.

A **Technical Drawing** is given for each project, outlining the shape of the furniture beneath the cover and indicating the sections to measure. The letters on the drawing link-up to the letters in Measuring Up and on the Cutting Layout.

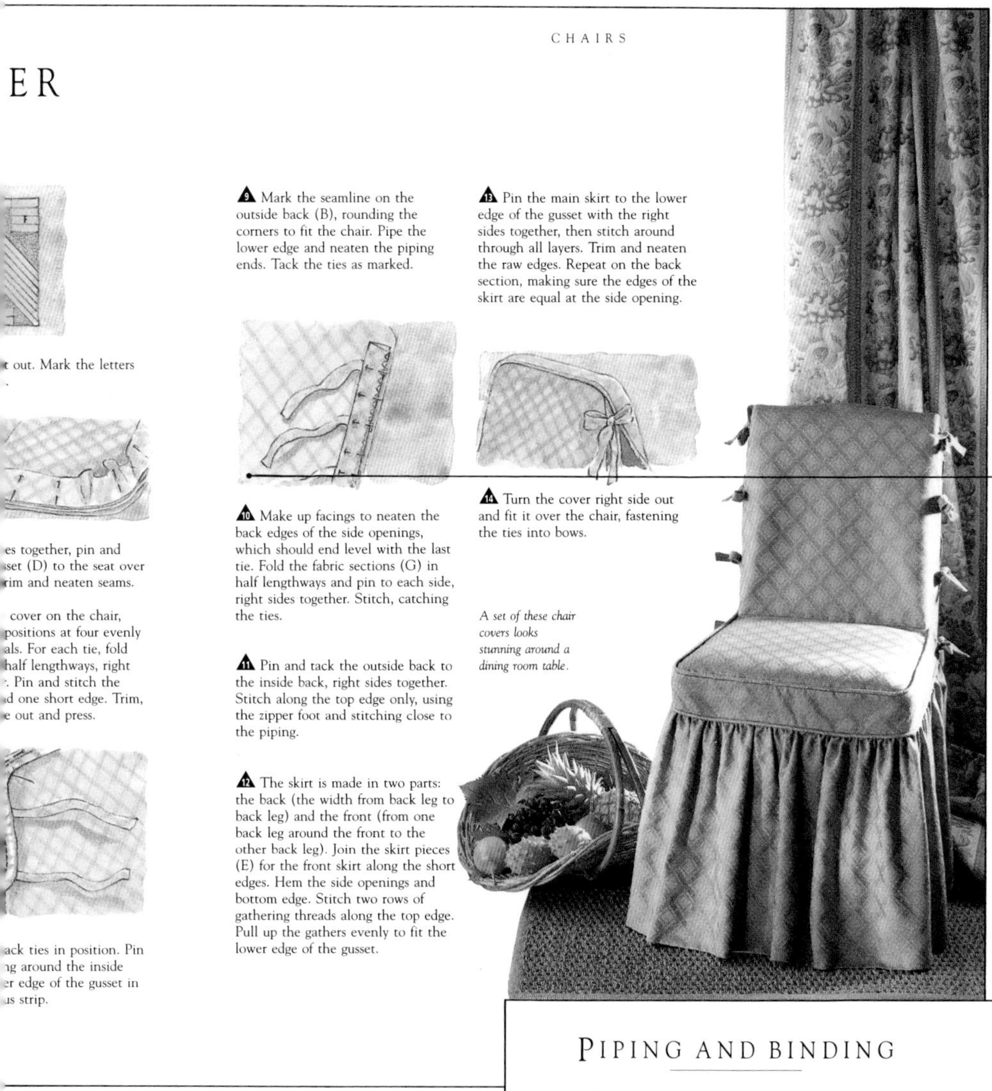

CHAIRS

ER

t out. Mark the letters

es together, pin and
sset (D) to the seat over
rim and neaten seams.

cover on the chair,
positions at four evenly
als. For each tie, fold
half lengthways, right
. Pin and stitch the
d one short edge. Trim,
e out and press.

ack ties in position. Pin
ng around the inside
er edge of the gusset in
as strip.

▲9 Mark the seamline on the outside back (B), rounding the corners to fit the chair. Pipe the lower edge and neaten the piping ends. Tack the ties as marked.

▲10 Make up facings to neaten the back edges of the side openings, which should end level with the last tie. Fold the fabric sections (G) in half lengthways and pin to each side, right sides together. Stitch, catching the ties.

▲11 Pin and tack the outside back to the inside back, right sides together. Stitch along the top edge only, using the zipper foot and stitching close to the piping.

▲12 The skirt is made in two parts: the back (the width from back leg to back leg) and the front (from one back leg around the front to the other back leg). Join the skirt pieces (E) for the front skirt along the short edges. Hem the side openings and bottom edge. Stitch two rows of gathering threads along the top edge. Pull up the gathers evenly to fit the lower edge of the gusset.

▲13 Pin the main skirt to the lower edge of the gusset with the right sides together, then stitch around through all layers. Trim and neaten the raw edges. Repeat on the back section, making sure the edges of the skirt are equal at the side opening.

▲14 Turn the cover right side out and fit it over the chair, fastening the ties into bows.

A set of these chair covers looks stunning around a dining room table.

Instructions for making the project are listed in step-by-step form and more difficult instructions are accompanied by illustrations.

Some of the more complex techniques are explained with step-by-step instructions and accompanied by illustrations.

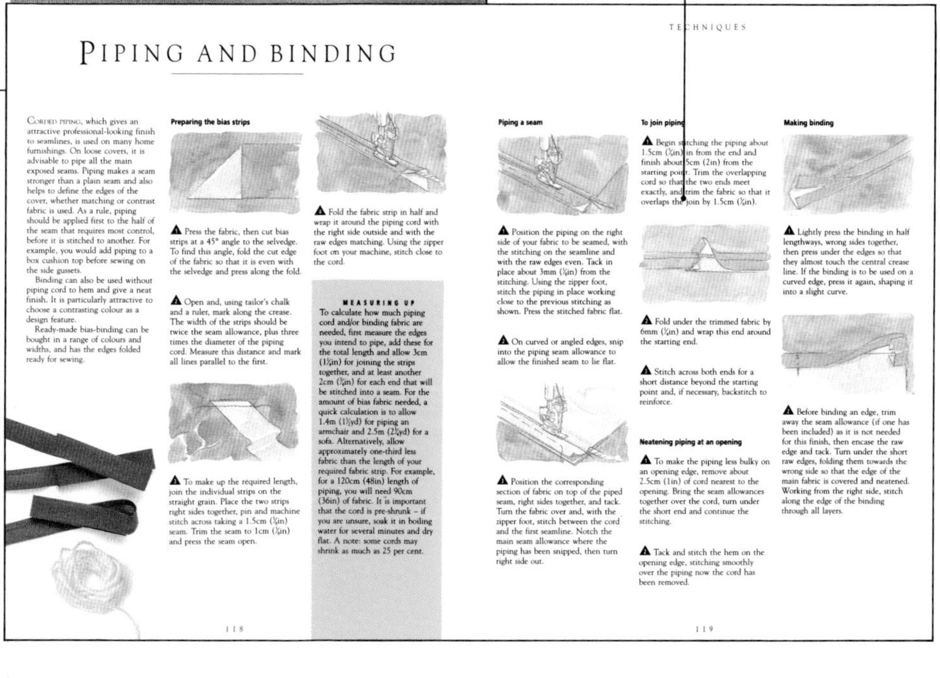

TECHNIQUES

PIPING AND BINDING

CORDED PIPING, which gives an attractive professional-looking finish to seamlines, is used on many home furnishings. On loose covers, it is advisable to pipe all the main exposed seams. Piping makes a seam stronger than a plain seam and also helps to define the edges of the cover, whether matching or contrast fabric is used. As a rule, piping should be applied first to the half of the seam that requires most control, before it is stitched to another. For example, you would add piping to a box cushion top before sewing on the side gussets.

Binding can also be used without piping cord to hem and give a neat finish. It is particularly attractive to choose a contrasting colour as a design feature.

Ready-made bias-binding can be bought in a range of colours and widths, and has the edges folded ready for sewing.

Preparing the bias strips

▲1 Press the fabric, then cut bias strips at a 45° angle to the selvedge. To find this angle, fold the cut edge of the fabric so that it is even with the selvedge and press along the fold.

▲2 Open and, using tailor's chalk and a ruler, mark along the crease. The width of the strips should be twice the seam allowance, plus three times the diameter of the piping cord. Measure this distance and mark all lines parallel to the first.

▲3 To make up the required length, join the individual strips on the straight grain. Place the two strips right sides together, pin and machine stitch across taking a 1.5cm (⅝in) seam. Trim the seam to 1cm (⅜in) and press the seam open.

▲4 Fold the fabric strip in half and wrap it around the piping cord with the right side outside and with the raw edges matching. Using the zipper foot on your machine, stitch close to the cord.

MEASURING UP

To calculate how much piping cord and/or binding fabric are needed, first measure the edges you intend to pipe, add these for the total length and allow 3cm (1¼in) for joining the strips together, and at least another 2cm (¾in) for each end that will be stitched into a seam. For the amount of bias fabric needed, a quick calculation is to allow 1.4m (1½yd) for piping an armchair and 2.5m (2¾yd) for a sofa. Alternatively, allow approximately one-third less fabric than the length of your required fabric strip. For example, for a 120cm (48in) length of piping, you will need 90cm (36in) of fabric. It is important that the cord is pre-shrunk – if you are unsure, soak it in boiling water for several minutes and dry flat. A note: some cords may shrink as much as 25 per cent.

118

Piping a seam

▲1 Position the piping on the right side of your fabric to be seamed, with the stitching on the seamline and with the raw edges even. Tack in place about 3mm (⅛in) from the stitching. Using the zipper foot, stitch the piping in place working close to the previous stitching as shown. Press the stitched fabric flat.

▲2 On curved or angled edges, snip into the piping seam allowance to allow the finished seam to lie flat.

▲3 Position the corresponding section of fabric on top of the piped seam, right sides together, and tack. Turn the fabric over and, with the zipper foot, stitch between the cord and the first seamline. Notch the main seam allowance where the piping has been snipped, then turn right side out.

To join piping

▲1 Begin stitching the piping about 1.5cm (⅝in) in from the end and finish about 5cm (2in) from the starting point. Trim the overlapping cord so that the two ends meet exactly, and trim the fabric so that it overlaps the join by 1.5cm (⅝in).

▲2 Fold under the trimmed fabric by 6mm (¼in) and wrap this end around the starting end.

▲3 Stitch across both ends for a short distance beyond the starting point and, if necessary, backstitch to reinforce.

Neatening piping at an opening

▲1 To make the piping less bulky on an opening edge, remove about 2.5cm (1in) of cord nearest to the opening. Bring the seam allowances together over the cord, turn under the short end and continue the stitching.

▲2 Tack and stitch the hem on the opening edge, stitching smoothly over the piping now the cord has been removed.

Making binding

▲1 Lightly press the binding in half lengthways, wrong sides together, then press under the edges so that they almost touch the central crease line. If the binding is to be used on a curved edge, press it again, shaping it into a slight curve.

▲2 Before binding an edge, trim away the seam allowance (if one has been included) as it is not needed for this finish, then encase the raw edge and tack. Turn under the short raw edges, folding them towards the wrong side so that the edge of the main fabric is covered and neatened. Working from the right side, stitch along the edge of the binding through all layers.

119

► A more detailed explanation of the techniques used in the projects can be found in the Techniques chapter. This can be used by both the novice to gain familiarity with new skills, and by the seasoned sewer needing to brush up on little-used techniques.

MEASURING UP

Once questions of design and style have been settled, the next element to determine is how much fabric is needed. To do this, you must take the measurements of the furniture being covered and this is called measuring up. The example that follows shows the general shapes and forms most likely to be covered, and while no two pieces of furniture are exactly alike, the principles of measuring up can be applied to any furniture. The important thing is to understand the principles.

NOTE
On an armchair, it will probably not be necessary to join pieces of fabric in order to make up the total width for a seat, but on a sofa the measurement will invariably be wider than the fabric. This also affects inside and outside back pieces. See Working with Fabric, pages 122–125, for more information on joining pieces for width.

Assemble the necessary tools: fabric measuring tape, paper and pencil. If you are working with furniture that already has a loose cover, remove it in order to take measurements of the furniture unhindered. **All loose cushions are measured and treated separately in this book but you do need to consider them when measuring and purchasing fabric.**

The main sections of a sofa or armchair are: the outside back, the inside back, the seat, the inside arm, the outside arm, the front arm, the border and usually the skirt. Covers with more sophisticated designs may have more pieces. The main measure of each piece includes its width taken at the widest point, and its depth taken at the deepest point. To this, you must add a seam allowance to the perimeter, which is a standard measure of 1.5cm ($\frac{5}{8}$in). Pieces that adjoin the back and sides of the seat section will have a tuck-in allowance as well, which has a standard measure of 15cm (6in).

The chart opposite gives an example of how to calculate the fabric quantity for some basic sections. In this book, we assign a letter to each piece; which includes the total measurement. For example, instructions for measuring the same seat piece in the chart opposite would read:

Seat – **Measure width and depth plus tuck-ins (C).**

All Measuring Up instructions begin with a general note on seam and tuck-in allowances so that they can be taken into account where required.

ANATOMY OF A LOOSE COVER

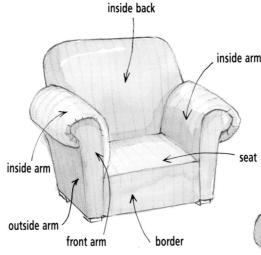

inside back

inside arm

inside arm

outside arm

front arm

border

seat

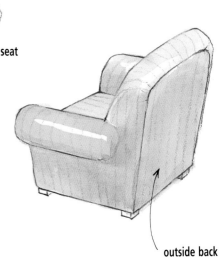

outside back

WHAT IS A TUCK-IN?
A tuck-in allowance is the extra fabric allowed for the crevices around the seat area – the place where loose change and other items often get trapped.

MEASURING UP CHARTS

The following charts illustrate the calculations you need to make when measuring a furniture section. The seat has tuck-ins on both width and depth sides, the inside back has a tuck-in on depth only, while the outside back has no tuck-ins. Floor-level pieces will need hem allowances.

Measuring the seat

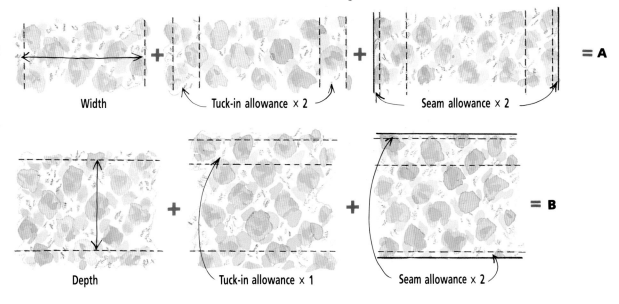

Width + Tuck-in allowance × 2 + Seam allowance × 2 = **A**

Depth + Tuck-in allowance × 1 + Seam allowance × 2 = **B**

Total fabric = A × B

Measuring the inside back

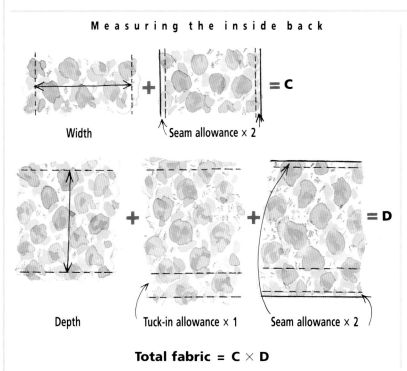

Width + Seam allowance × 2 = **C**

Depth + Tuck-in allowance × 1 + Seam allowance × 2 = **D**

Total fabric = C × D

Measuring the outside back

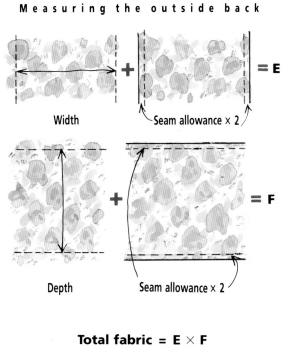

Width + Seam allowance × 2 = **E**

Depth + Seam allowance × 2 = **F**

Total fabric = E × F

FURNITURE TYPES

The following are guidelines for measuring some of the more common furniture shapes. Once you have mastered the techniques of measuring up, you can apply them to any piece of furniture you want to cover. For piping cord and bias strips, measure all the seams to be piped, following the project instructions. As a rule, allow 1.4m (1½yd) of fabric for the bias strips to pipe seams on armchairs and 2.5m (2¾yd) for sofas, see Piping and Binding pages 118–119.

Scroll-armed furniture

With this shape, sections are taken over the tops of the scroll and seamed at the outside, where the scroll ends. The design usually incorporates tucks.

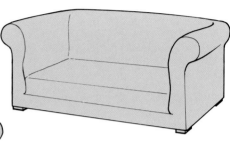

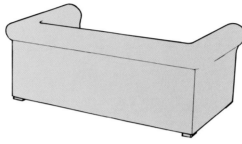

Outside back – Measure the width across the back and add seam allowances at both sides. Measure the depth from the top edge to the bottom (if there is no skirt, this measure extends to floor level) and add seam allowances (A).
Inside back – Measure the width above the arms (the widest point) and across the scroll to the outside back edge. Measure the depth from the outside back edge across the box-side to the base of the seat, adding a seam allowance at the top and a tuck-in allowance at the bottom (B).
Seat – Measure the width at the widest point and add tuck-ins at both sides. Measure the depth and add a tuck-in at the back edge and a seam allowance at the front (C).
Border – Measure the width from the edges of the arm gussets and add seam allowances. Measure the depth from the edge of the seat to the bottom (if there is no skirt, this measure extends to floor level) and add seam allowances (D).

Inside arm – Measure the width at the widest point and add seam allowances. Measure the depth from the outside arm edge, over the scroll and down to the seat, adding a seam allowance at the top and a tuck-in at the bottom (E).
Outside arm – Measure the width and add seam allowances at both sides. Measure the depth from underneath the scroll at the top to the bottom (if there is no skirt, this measure extends to floor level) and add seam allowances (F).
Front arm – Measure width and add seam allowances. Measure the depth from top to bottom (if there is no skirt, this measure extends to floor level) and add seam allowances (G).
Skirt – Measure the perimeter at the base and add an allowance for opening hems and joining pieces to make up the total width. Measure the depth and add one seam and one hem allowance. Skirts with gathers or pleats will require additional fabric for fullness, see Frills and Pleats pages 120–21.

Upright chair with upholstery

To accommodate the depth of the padding and/or struts the inside back and seat measures extend back and down, respectively. When assembling, these pieces usually require darts for the excess fabric.

Outside back – Measure the depth from the top of the chair to the top seat level plus seam allowance. Measure the width across the back, plus seam allowances and hems for openings, if required (A).
Inside back – Measure the depth from the top of the chair where it meets the outside back, allowing for the depth of the padding seam, and add allowances. Measure the width across the back to the outside edges and add seam allowances (B).
Seat – Measure the depth plus seam allowances, and the width plus seam allowances (C).
Skirt – Measure the perimeter at the base and add an allowance for joining pieces to make up the total width. Measure the depth and add one seam and one hem allowance. Skirts with gathers or pleats will require additional fabric for fullness, see Frills and Pleats pages 120–21 (D).

Folding chair

The measures shown here are for a cover with a seam in the middle of the inside and outside back point. If your chair struts are deep, you may want to extend either the inside or outside back to accommodate them.

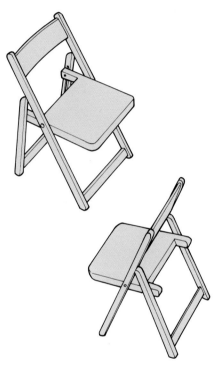

Outside back – Measure the width across the back legs and add seam allowances. Measure the depth from the top to the floor, adding a seam and a hem allowance (A).
Inside back – Measure the width, meeting the outside back, and add seam allowances. Measure the depth, also meeting the outside back, and add seam allowances (B).
Seat – Measure the width and add seam allowances; measure the depth and add seam allowances. You will also need an easing allowance of about 2.5cm (1in) (C).
Skirt – Measure as for upright chair with upholstery, see left.

Ottoman

There are two skirt options here. We have shown the top panel extending down the sides, but you could also raise the skirt to meet the top panel at the edges.

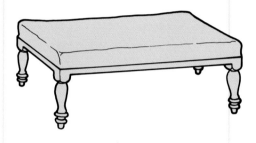

Top panel – Measure the width from one side to the other, extending down the sides to meet the padding, and add seam allowances. Repeat for the length (A).
Skirt – Measure the perimeter where the top of the skirt meets the top panel. Before adding seam allowances, determine the style, such as mock or inverted pleats, and add the necessary allowances (see Frills and Pleats pages 120–21) Measure the depth from the top of the skirt line to the floor, plus allowances for one seam and one hem (B).

CUTTING LAYOUTS

Once you have obtained the measures for each piece of your cover, you can prepare your cutting layout, which is a scaled-down plan of how the pieces can be organized on a length of fabric. This is important because it is the step that tells you how much fabric to buy. Unless otherwise specified, all projects in this book have been calculated using the standard fabric width of 122cm (48in).

NOTE
Do not count the selvedge edges – the finished lengthwise edge – in your calculations. Although it is tempting to use them to avoid neatening edges, they are more tightly woven than the actual fabric and, if used, the seams of your finished cover may pucker.

The cutting layouts for each project have been calculated for you **but they are just guides**. How your pieces fall on the fabric depends on the size of your chair, so you will need to make your own cutting layout adapted to the measurements of your furniture. **Always remember to allow for cushion covers when calculating layouts.**

2 Transfer your measuring up information to the graph paper. As an example, we have added sample

3 The remaining pieces of your cover can be calculated and transferred to graph paper in the same way. Label each piece as you go and mark the top of each piece as

1 To calculate the cutting layout you will need graph paper, a pencil and a calculator. Assign a measurement value to each square of your graph paper, for example, 1 square = 10cm (4in).

measures to the seat measurement chart, see opposite.

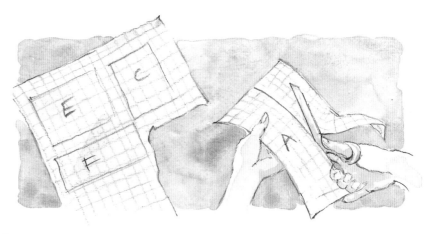

well as the straight grain of the fabric (do this with a lengthways arrow) so that the point goes in the same direction. Cut out each piece.

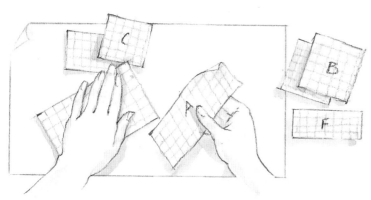

6 Convert back to the original measurements to obtain the actual amount of fabric to purchase.

4 Next, arrange side by side on a scaled down length of fabric drawn on graph paper to the same scale (1 square = 10cm/4in). The goal is to arrange the pieces so that you use the minimum amount of fabric and keep lengthways arrows parallel to the straight grain. Remember to allow for extras like bows or bias strips for piping, see Piping and Binding pages 118–119.

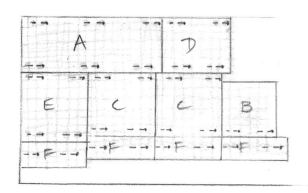

5 This cutting layout has been drawn for an upright chair cover with mock pleats at each corner. This is the ideal layout for a solid fabric but pattern placement might need repositioning if you are using fabric with a motif.

7 The next stage is to buy your fabric and transfer the scaled up measures, see Working with Fabric, pages 122–125. Before marking your measurements, lay the fabric on the furniture to check position and verify against your cutting layout. This is especially crucial with patterned or striped fabrics.

MATCHING MOTIFS AND STRIPES

It is important to choose your fabric prior to making your cutting layout so that you know the actual width and whether to allow for patterns. As a rule, allow for at least one repeat per pattern section (or panels when joining widths) with large-patterned motif fabrics and horizontal stripes. See also Working with Fabrics pages 122–123 and Hand Stitching pages 112–113. If you are a beginner sewer it is advisable to start with an overall small print.

SEAT MEASUREMENT CHART

40cm (16in) wide	+	5cm (2in)	+	30cm (12in)
		Seam allowance × 2		Tuck-in allowance × 2
40cm (16in) deep	+	5cm (2in)	+	15cm (6in)
		Seam allowance × 2		Tuck-in allowance × 1

The seat is a piece of fabric that measures 75cm (30in) wide by 60cm (24in) deep.

Seven steps to successful loose covers

The following checklist discusses seven important stages involved in planning and preparing for the projects. These stages are designed to help you make the best choice of fabric and style of cover to suit your particular needs.

1

CO-ORDINATING YOUR INTERIOR

Making your own loose covers offers endless scope to match existing colour schemes and fabrics, thus creating a totally co-ordinated furnishing style in your home.

Individuality

With the availability of so many styles and the wide range of attractive fabrics, it is also possible to give individual treatments to any room in the house, and even out of the house.

Similarly, by fitting a matching loose cover, individual chairs, chests and stools can easily be integrated into a furnishing scheme.

Making changes

Loose covers can be used in the living or dining room, to enliven the existing decor or to play an active role in a completely new decorating scheme. In children's rooms, they can be used as a simple solution to the evolving decor needs of a growing child by changing the covers as he or she develops different needs. Outside, loose covers can perk up old or rusty garden furniture, or they can dress-up furniture for a special outdoor occasion, such as a wedding.

2

CHOOSE A LOOK

Formal

Essentially, formal loose covers are made from classic fabrics such as satin, silk and damask, usually in subdued colours and in a tailored style with appropriately placed trims – piping, fringing and tassels – and entail a high degree of style and finish.

These covers have a timeless elegance, and if well made in high-quality fabric, they should withstand years of wear and the passing of fashion trends.

Semi-formal

Semi-formal covers allow for the use of more colourful patterned fabrics such as furnishing-weight linens, cottons and chintzes in less tailored styles, which can include pleated and gathered skirts, flounces and ruching.

This type of loose cover is a popular choice for any room and any time of year, encompassing the widest range of furniture styles and settings.

Informal

Informal loose covers may be made simply from fabrics with a home-spun look such as mattress ticking, gingham checks, floral patterns and novelty prints in plain, unstructured or gently gathered styles.

These covers are easy-to-make and easy to live with, and they allow you the opportunity to change them with your mood or with the seasons.

3

ORGANIZATION

A well-organized work space is essential for best results when handling large amounts of fabric for furniture and several loose cushions. As well as the fabric and furniture, allow space for your work table, ironing board, sewing machine and work basket. These should all be easily accessible.

You will need plenty of space around your piece of furniture since you will be constantly moving around it for measuring, shaping the fabric and fitting the cover. Fabric will inevitably fall on the floor so a clean floor is also essential. Prepare your list of requirements and assemble them in advance.

The furniture

It is best to remove all loose cushions and covers from the furniture right down to the basic upholstery, so that you can take exact measurements of each section. Hand-brush or vacuum the surfaces and especially in the crevices around the seat. Check that the framework and upholstery are sound. With older furniture, now is the time to inspect the under-frame for woodworm, and treat if necessary.

4

THE FABRIC

Wearability

For maximum wear, choose a soft-furnishing fabric which is recommended for loose covers by the manufacturer. It should be closely woven, tough, colour fast and pre-shrunk.

Handling

It is best to avoid thick fabrics as these can be difficult to work with, particularly on piped seams. For this reason, make sure your sewing machine is powerful enough to cope with the thicknesses of the fabrics you want to use.

Plain and patterned

For obvious reasons, it is easier (and more economical) to work with plain fabrics or those with small all-over patterns. Fabrics with large repeats and those with broad stripes, require extra attention when positioning and matching pieces. Extra fabric must be allowed.

5

MEASURING UP

Once you have decided on the style of loose cover and the type of fabric you would like to use, you will then need to find out how much fabric is required. You can calculate the total figure by taking the measurements of each section of your piece of furniture. Use a fabric tape measure to fit the contours of the upholstery, and write down the dimensions of each section, measuring across the widest points both horizontally and vertically and adding seam and hem allowances. This step is explained in detail in the previous section, pages 20–21.

Paper patterns

Make paper patterns for curved or complicated shapes using dressmaker's graph paper or ordinary wrapping paper and trace around the shape, directly from the furniture. Allow seam allowances before cutting out. Position the paper pattern onto its reserved fabric section and cut out.

Templates

Should you wish to position the same motif on the front arms of a sofa, for example, first cut out one rectangle of fabric to the required size (from a single layer) and, using it as a template, place it on the same motif. Turn the pattern piece over to get a mirror image and match it exactly before cutting out.

6

CUTTING LAYOUTS

Transfer the measurements obtained from measuring up to a scaled cutting layout which will show the square or rectangular shape of each reserved fabric section, and give the total amount of fabric needed.

Use a ruler and tailor's chalk to transfer all straight measurements to the wrong side of your fabric. If the pattern repeat does not show through on the wrong side, mark the right side but label each section on the wrong side. This will be the side facing when you are fitting and shaping the fabric sections on the furniture, so you will need to see the labels easily. Place paper patterns in position either directly on the uncut fabric or on the appropriate cut-out rectangle, pinning them on the straight grain before cutting out. Label in the same way. Each section is cut out separately ready for fitting and shaping on the furniture prior to machine stitching.

7

SEWING THE COVER

For large pieces of furniture, mark the centre lines with chalk and do the same on the fabric pieces. Match up any motifs and join together pieces to make up the width if necessary. Transfer the paper shape patterns to the fabric and cut out.

When you begin sewing, work carefully and in long uninterrupted stretches, if possible. When you do stop mid-project, try to organize your time so that you end at a logical break. It will be easier to carry on when you come back to the cover.

If you are unsure, make the cover in a test fabric, such as inexpensive curtain lining or even an old sheet, before you actually cut into your furnishing fabric.

SOFAS & ARMCHAIRS

Giving your sofas and armchairs a new look is not such a daunting task. Whether your cover is traditional or modern, the basic techniques are the same. This chapter offers many options and styles to suit even the beginner sewer. Whether you are redecorating or just want a new look for a new season, you'll find it here.

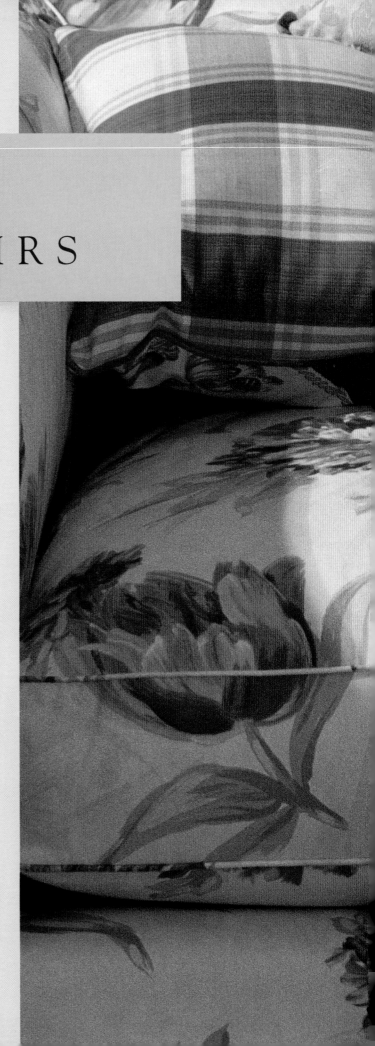

TRADITIONAL SOFA COVER

The curves on this sofa make careful fitting important.

CHECKLIST

Materials

closely woven furnishing fabric and lining
touch-and-close fastening
pre-shrunk piping cord
general sewing equipment   page 110–11

Techniques

patterned fabrics	page 122–25
securing and fastening	page 116–17
piping and binding	page 118–19

Measuring up

Add 1.5cm (⅝in) seam allowances, and 15cm (6in) tuck-ins where required:

Outside back – Measure width and depth (A).
Inside back – Measure width and the depth from scroll to seat plus tuck-in (B).
Seat – Measure width and depth, plus tuck-ins (C).
Border – Measure width and depth (D).
Inside arms – Measure width and depth from scroll to seat plus tuck-in (E).
Outside arms – Measure width and depth (F).
Front arms – Measure width and depth (G).
Skirt – Measure perimeter and depth plus hem (H); allow fabric and lining.
Mock pleats – Allow four pieces in fabric and lining (I).
Piping – Allow for bias strips (J).
Box cushion covers – See Index.

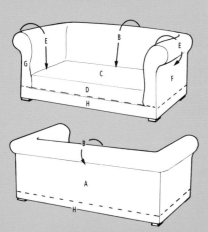

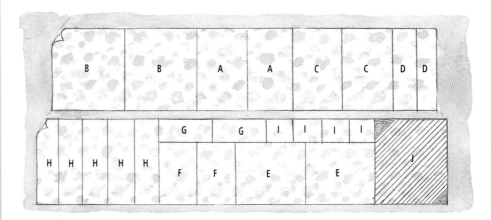

1 Using your measurements, mark the cutting lines on the grain of the fabric and cut out. Mark the letters on each piece.

2 To allow for the width of the sofa, the fabric will need to be joined across the outside and inside back (A and B), the seat (C) and the border (D). Place a full width piece of fabric in the centre of each section. Then, matching any pattern, join the necessary fabric widths at each side to make up the total width measurement.

3 Make up enough piping to fit all the required seams. On this sofa, the piped seams are: around both front arms, the top edge of the skirt, the seams joining the inside arm to the inside back and across the mitred corner to the back of the rolled edge.

4 On the sofa, mark a chalk line down the centre of the outside back, the inside back, the seat and the border. Repeat on the wrong side of the corresponding fabric sections.

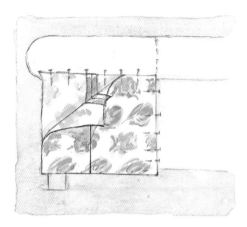

5 With the wrong sides together, fold the outside back (A) in half. Pin the fold to the sofa, lining up the centre marks. Smooth the fabric out to one side and pin again at the side seams and under the top rolled edge. Open up and pin at the other side.

6 Position the inside back (B) in the same way, with the tuck-in at the lower edge. Pin in place, shaping around the rolled top edge. On the back, use pleats to fit around the shape. Carefully cut the curve over the arm, extending the fabric outwards at the bottom to the full width of the tuck-in allowance.

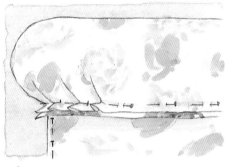

7 Right sides together, pin the inside back (B) to the outside back (A) along the seamlines. Clip into the seam allowance on the curves if necessary. Mark the seamline with chalk, marking between pins. Take out the holding pins and remove from the sofa.

8 Trim the seam allowance where necessary to 1.5cm (⅝in). On the inside back, pin piping along the inner back seam, including the tuck-in, and into the corner seam of the rolled top edge. Tack just inside the chalk line.

The piping extends diagonally from the inside back to the outside over the rolled edge.

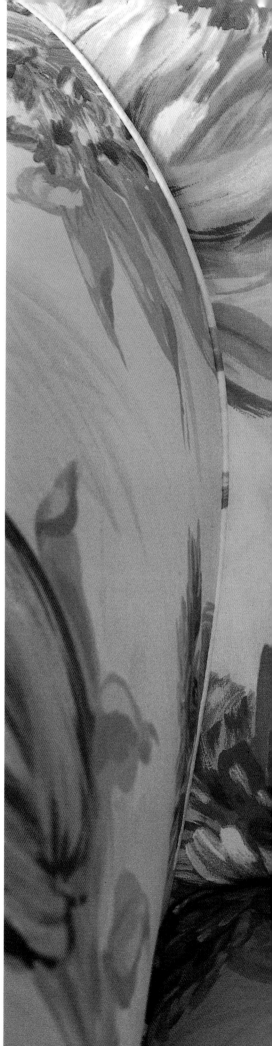

JOINING PATTERNED FABRICS

To make fabric sections wide enough for a sofa, for example, half fabric widths are stitched to each side of one full width. Patterned or striped fabrics are tacked together so that the pattern matches at the seam, not the cut edge.

To begin, work from the right side and press under the seam allowance on one piece of fabric. Lay this piece over the other so that the pattern matches exactly, then pin. Using the ladder stitch (see pages 112–113), tack the pieces together from the right side. Finally, machine stitch the seam from the wrong side and press the turnings to one side.

9 Replace the cover. Right sides together, position the seat (C) as in step 5. Allow for the tuck-in along the sides and back of the seat, then pin to the inside back. Mark the seamlines. Remove from the sofa and trim the seam allowance. Tack, then stitch the back seam.

10 In the same way, pin and mark the outside arms (F) and the inside arms (E) in place, wrong side out. Be sure that the seam falls just below the rolled edge of the arm. Tack and stitch together. Cut and clip the curve over the inner arm, extending it outwards on the bottom to the width of the seat tuck-in.

11 Arrange the excess fabric around the front edge of the arm into small even pleats about 5cm (2in) deep. Pin and with tacking stitches tack to secure. Mark a guideline to help shape the curved front arm. Trim the seam allowance.

12 Pin the tuck-in along the lower edge of the inside arms to the tuck-in edges of the seat to hold in place.

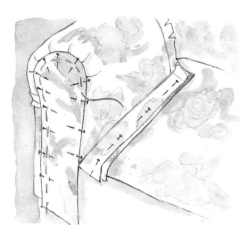

13 Position the front arm (G). Mark the seamline and trim but do not notch the seam allowance. Tack piping around the front arm seams, right sides together. Tack and stitch the front arms in place.

14 Replace the inside back, seat and arm sections on the sofa, wrong side out. Pin to the sofa to hold in place. Arrange so that the tapered edges of the inside arms and inside back form a mitred corner across the rolled edge. Tack, stitch and neaten the seams. Stitch the outside and the inside back seams under the rolled edge.

15 Replace the cover wrong side out, then push in the tuck-in allowance at the back and the sides of the seat. Mark a line on each side section at the top of the tuck-in. Pull out the tuck-in allowance and pin the inner arm tuck-in to the seat side tuck-in, matching the chalked lines. Where necessary, trim the tuck-in allowance below the chalked line to 15cm (6in). Re-pin and stitch the tuck-in seams.

16 Replace the cover right side out, with the seam allowance protruding at the front edge. Pin the border to the front of the seat section and to the seam allowance of the tuck-in, wrong sides together. Pin the sides of the border to the front arms below the seat tuck-in. Trim the seams. Remove, re-pin and stitch with right sides together.

17 Replace the cover right side out. Pin the seamlines where the outside back meets the outside arms. Mark one seamline for the opening including about 8cm (3in) into the rolled edge. Remove and trim. Pin, tack and stitch one seam, leaving the other side open. Trim to 2.5cm (1in). Neaten all seams.

18 Along the edges of the opening, turn under a double hem. Pin, then tack in place. Pin one section of the fastening to the wrong side of the back opening edge and the corresponding piece to the wrong side of the front opening edge. Tack, then stitch. Press the seam allowance towards the arm and stitch across the top of the opening to hold.

Evenly spaced darts accentuate the scroll arms.

19 For the skirt, replace the cover on the sofa, right side out. Calculate the top position (the lower edge should reach about 1.5cm (⅝in) above the floor), then add a 2cm (¾in) seam allowance below this point. Using pins, mark a line around the cover at this level and trim.

20 Pin a continuous length of piping to the right side of the lower edge of the cover, with a 1.5cm (⅝in) seam allowance. Beginning at the back opening, tack in place.

21 Join together both skirt and lining widths as in step 2, making up separate sections for long and short sides. With right sides together, pin one skirt section to one skirt lining section. Tack and stitch around the two short sides and along the lower long side. Turn right side out and press. Repeat on the remaining sections, checking that the edges of each skirt section meet the adjacent section evenly at the corners.

22 Pin each skirt section to the main cover over the piping, right sides together, then tack.

23 Make the mock corner pleats as in step 21.

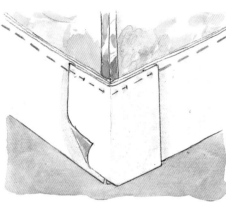

24 Replace the cover wrong side out. Pin each mock corner pleat to the back of the skirt at each corner. On the opening corner, position the mock pleat in the same way but attach only one half in place. Remove and tack.

25 Starting from the opening corner, stitch the skirt to the cover and neaten the edges. Neaten the unfixed raw edge of the half-stitched mock pleat. Attach one section of the fastening to the front of the unfixed pleat edge and the other section to the corresponding position on the back of the skirt.

26 Make up the cushion covers, checking that any repeat in the fabric pattern lines up with the inside back and border sections. Include piping in the top and bottom edges of the gusset seams.

Be sure to match up motifs as evenly as possible, especially when working with large-motif fabrics. The beginner sewer will find it easier to work with a small-motif fabric, which hides miscalculations much better.

ARMCHAIR COVER

This cover features diagonal seams and angled skirt corners.

CHECKLIST

Materials

closely woven cotton furnishing fabric
pre-shrunk piping cord
zip and touch-and-close fasteners
general sewing equipment   page 110–11

Techniques

piping and binding   page 118–19
inserting a zip   page 116–17

Measuring up

Add 1.5cm (⅝in) seam allowances and 15cm (6in) tuck-in allowances where indicated:
Outside back – Measure the depth to the top of the skirt and the width (A).
Inside back – Measure the depth plus tuck-in and the width (B).
Seat – Measure width and depth, plus tuck-ins for sides and the back edge (C).
Border – Measure width and depth (D).
Inside arm – Measure width and depth, plus tuck-ins for both inside edges (E).
Outside arm – Measure width and depth (F).
Front arm – Measure width and depth (G).
Skirt – Measure width and depth on all four sides and allow for double thickness (H).
Mock pleats – Allow four pieces (I).
Piping – Allow for bias strips (J).
Box cushion covers – See Index.

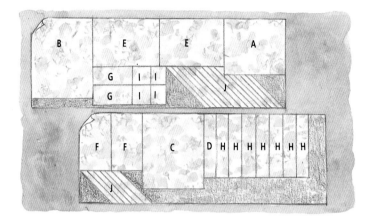

1 Using your measurements, mark the cutting lines on the grain of the fabric as shown and cut out. Mark the letters on each piece.

2 Make up sufficient piping to trim the exposed seams. Our piped seams are: around the front arms, the top edge of the skirt, and the sides and top of the outside back and the box cushion.

3 Mark a centre line down the outside back, inside back, seat and border of the chair. Do the same on the wrong sides of the corresponding pieces of fabric.

5 Pin the inside back (B) as in step 4, allowing for the tuck-ins. Mark the back seamline. Cut the curve over the arm, tapering it towards the width of the lower tuck-in. Notch seam allowances over curves until the fabric lies flat.

4 Fold the outside back (A) in half, wrong sides together. Pin the fold to the centre line on the chair, smooth out the fabric and re-pin the edges. Mark the seamlines.

6 To shape the shoulders, pin and tack tucks as shown. Pin the two sections (A and B) right sides together, then trim seam allowances.

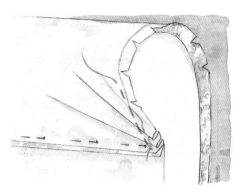

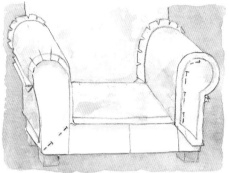

7 Position the inside arms (E) wrong side out, then taper and notch the inner arm back seam to match the inside back (B). Pin the outside (F) and inside arms together, wrong side out, with the seam just under the rolled edge. To shape, arrange tucks under the front arm and tack to secure. Notch the curves, mark the seamlines and trim.

8 Tack and stitch first the outside arm seam, then stitch the inside arm to the inside back in a continuous seam, taking it diagonally over the arm towards the back edge.

9 Replace the cover wrong side out. Position the seat (C) wrong side out, centre lines matching. Mark tuck-ins to correspond with inside back and inside arm sections. Trim tuck-ins, then pin and stitch.

10 Replace the cover wrong side out. Position the front arms (G), wrong side out, first marking the diagonal seam on the chair with pins. Pin the front arms in place. Mark the seamline from the outside skirt level, across the diagonal line and around the curve of the arm. Trim seam allowances but do not notch. Push down the tuck-ins and pin the lower front arms to the inside arm tuck-ins.

11 Remove all the pins and tack piping to the sides and top of the outside back and the front arms, starting and finishing at the diagonal outside point.

12 Stitch the remaining seams, pressing all turnings away from the front of the chair as you stitch. Leave an opening at the back by stitching to within 10cm (4in) of the arm.

Piping strengthens seams and adds design detail.

13 Replace the cover right side out. Push down tuck-ins and position the border (D) right side out. Mark and trim the seam allowances. Pin to the seat front and tuck-in, then the seam across the front arm. Remove, re-pin and stitch, right sides together.

14 Replace the cover and pin-mark the skirt position. Trim excess fabric. Pipe around the bottom edge.

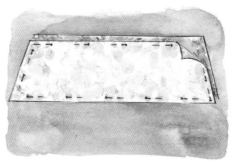

15 Mark and trim the seam allowances on the skirt sections (G), angling the corners to follow the seamline on the front arms. Pin, then stitch only the sides and bottom edge, right sides together.

A long opening makes it easier to get the cover on and off.

16 Trim the corners of the skirts, turn right side out and press. Insert the zip at the opening.

17 Replace the cover wrong side out. Pin the skirt in place. Hem all but one long edge of each mock corner piece (I). Pin one to each corner over the skirt, raw edges matching. Pin one half only on the opening edge. Remove cover, then tack and stitch.

18 Stitch the touch-and-close fastening to the mock pleat at the opening edge and at the corresponding point on the cover. Make up the cushion covers.

When making a tailored cover, choose a fabric that is strong but easy to work with and has year-round appeal.

MODERN SOFA COVER

A gathered skirt softens the
lines of this cover.

CHECKLIST

Materials

closely woven furnishing fabric
pre-shrunk piping cord
fastenings: hook-and-eye tape, press
   fasteners, touch-and-close tape
general sewing equipment   page 110–11

Techniques

patterned fabrics   page 122–25
securing and fastening   page 116–17
piping and binding   page 118–19

Measuring up

Add 1.5cm (⅝in) seam allowances and 15cm
(6in) tuck-ins where required:
Outside back – Measure width and depth (A).
Inside back – Measure width and the depth
plus tuck-in (B).
Seat – Measure width and the depth plus
tuck-in (C).
Border – Measure width and depth (D).
Inside arms – Measure width and the depth
plus tuck-in (E).
Outside arms – Measure width and depth (F).
Arm gussets – Measure width and depth (G).
Skirt – Measure depth plus hem allowance
and the perimeter at the base, plus half total
measurement for gathered fullness (H).
Piping – Allow for bias strips (I).
Box cushion covers – See Index.

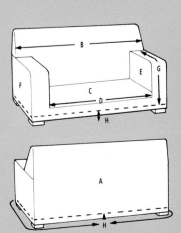

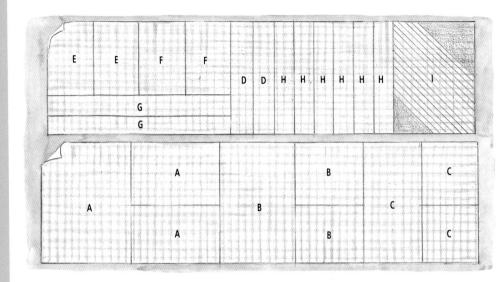

1 Using your measurements, mark
the cutting lines on the grain of the
fabric. Cut out and mark the letters
on each piece.

2 You will need to join lengths of
fabric to allow for the width of the
sofa. This affects the outside back
(A), inside back (B), seat (C) and
border (D) sections. Place the full
width of fabric in the centre of each
section. Matching any pattern, pin
and stitch narrower widths to either
side to make up the total width.

3 Make up sufficient piping for all
the required seams. Here, the piped
seams are: the back above the arms,
the inside edge of the arm gussets,
the front and top edge of the outside
arms, and all around the base (the
top of the skirt).

4 Using tailor's chalk, mark the
centre of the outside back, inside
back, seat and border on the sofa.
Do the same on the corresponding
fabric sections.

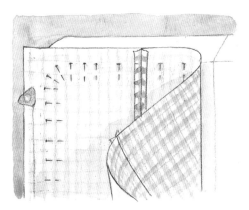

5 Centre lines matching, pin the outside back (A) to the sofa wrong side out. Using tailor's chalk, mark the seamlines along the top edge of the outside back and down the sides.

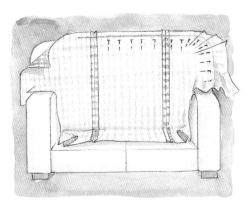

6 Repeat step 5 for the inside back (B), allowing for the tuck-in along the lower edge. On the shoulders, ease in fullness or neaten into darts and tack to secure.

7 Pin pieces A and B together down the side. Cut the angle over the arm, snip into the corners, then taper the remaining fabric along the inside arm to the width of the lower tuck-in.

8 Remove the back sections and trim the seam allowance to 1.5cm (⅝in). Tack piping around the sides and top of the outside back. Pin and stitch the seams as far as the arms and neaten the edges.

When working with striped fabrics, be sure that all the sections are cut so that the lines run straight on the finished cover.

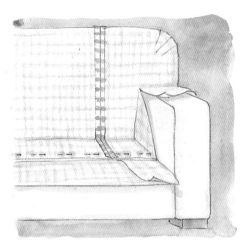

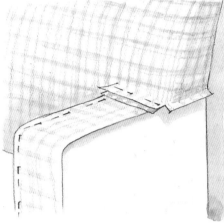

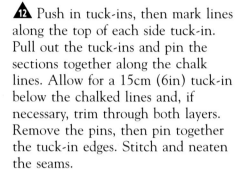

12 Push in tuck-ins, then mark lines along the top of each side tuck-in. Pull out the tuck-ins and pin the sections together along the chalk lines. Allow for a 15cm (6in) tuck-in below the chalked lines and, if necessary, trim through both layers. Remove the pins, then pin together the tuck-in edges. Stitch and neaten the seams.

9 Replace the cover and repeat step 5 for the seat section (C), making a tuck-in along the back and side edges. Trim the fabric and pin the edges of the back tuck-ins together. Stitch and neaten the seams.

10 Replace the stitched cover wrong side out. Pin the arm gussets (G) in position. Mark the seamlines and trim the seams. Apply piping to the right side of the inside long edge. Replace the arm gussets, wrong side out. Pin to the inside back and stitch.

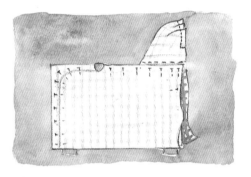

13 Pin the outside arm (F) to the outside back and the arm gusset and mark the seamlines. Mark one back seam for the opening, about 10cm (4in) above the arm, unpicking the back seam on the opening side. Trim the seam allowance.

SHAPED BOX CUSHION COVERS

- Make a pattern from paper using the old cushion cover or the cushion itself as a template. Place it on the paper, draw around the shape, add seam allowances and cut out. Using the pattern, cut out one top piece and one bottom piece for each cover.
- For the gusset, take measurements following the instructions on page 78 (and see below) and cut out the gusset pieces.
- Following the same instructions, continue to make up the cushion covers incorporating piping in the top and bottom edges and a zip fastener in the back gusset.

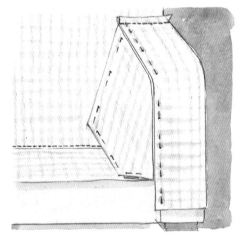

11 Replace the cover wrong side out. Pin the inside arms (E) to the inside back. Taper the seamline from a 15cm (6in) tuck-in to a normal seam allowance where the seams meet the arm gussets at the top, to match the inside back.

14 On the outside arm, pipe the arm gusset edges, right sides together, taking the piping through to the back corner. Stitch the arm gusset and inside back to the outside arm, right sides together and neaten, leaving the back opening unstitched. Trim the allowance on the opening to 2.5cm (1in). Along the sides of the back opening, turn under a double hem.

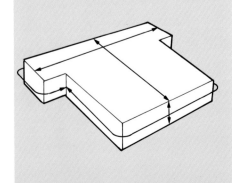

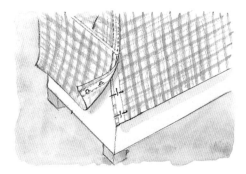

17 For the skirt, replace the cover right side out. Calculate the position for the top of the skirt, with a 2cm (¾in) seam allowance, then mark with pins. Trim.

15 Pin and tack fastening to the cover. Press the seam allowance towards the arm. Topstitch across the top of the opening.

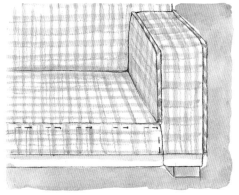

18 Remove the cover, then pipe the lower edge, beginning and ending at the back opening and taking a 1.5cm (⅝in) seam allowance.

16 Replace the cover right side out. Tuck-in the seat sides and back, leaving the seam allowance protruding at the front edge. Position and pin the border (D) to the seat and to the seam allowance of the tuck-in with wrong sides together. Pin it to the front arms below the seat tuck-in. Trim the seams. Remove and re-pin with right sides together, then stitch.

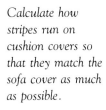

Calculate how stripes run on cushion covers so that they match the sofa cover as much as possible.

TUCK-INS

When making a cover for an upholstered sofa or armchair, you will find that tuck-ins are required. These are large fabric allowances on certain sections of the cover – all those that share a seam with the seat – which are pushed into the crevices of the upholstery to help prevent strain. They are needed at points where movement occurs when the furniture is sat upon; such as where the inside back meets the arms and seat, for instance, and where the inner arms meet the sides of the seat.

Tuck-in allowances for the seat are usually 15cm (6in) deep, whereas those around the inner arm and inside back may be narrower since they are usually shaped or tapered to fit. As the cover is being made, the edges of adjoining tuck-ins are stitched together to form a kind of pocket. On the finished cover, it is these pockets that are pushed deep into the crevices of the furniture.

In fitting the cover, a thin (but strong) piece of cardboard or a clean wooden spatula is useful for pushing the tuck-ins in place.

19 Join the short sides of the skirt sections (H) to form a continuous length. Press the seams open. Turn under a narrow double hem, plus double hems down the two short sides for the back opening.

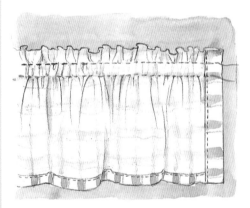

20 On the top edge, make two rows of gathering stitches 12mm ($\frac{1}{2}$in) inside the seam allowance. Pull up the gathers until the skirt is the required width. Stitch through the gathers to hold in place.

21 With the right sides together, pin the skirt to the main cover, then tack. Stitch close to the piping with the zipper foot.

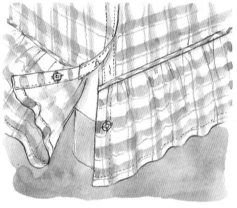

22 Attach the press fastener to each side of the skirt opening. To emphasize the smooth lines of the sofa front, attach pieces of touch-and-close fastening to the sofa and cover just above the skirt.

23 Make box cushion covers following the instructions on page 78.

Contrasting throw cushions add to the appeal of the cover.

EASY SLIP-ON-SKIRT COVER

Simple to make, this cover adapts best to square-shaped chairs and small sofas.

CHECKLIST

Materials

cotton furnishing fabric, 140cm (55in) wide
elastic
general sewing equipment   page 110–11

Techniques

patterned fabric   page 122–25

Measuring up

To the following measurements, add 1.5cm (⅝in) for all seam allowances:

Main cover – Measure the depth from floor level centre front to floor level centre outside back, plus 30cm (12in) for tuck-in; measure the width from floor level on both sides plus 30cm (12in) tuck-in (A).

Skirt – Measure length around the base of the chair and add half total measurement for gathered fullness, and measure the depth plus hem allowance (B).

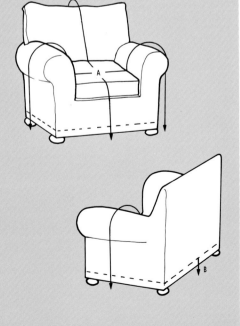

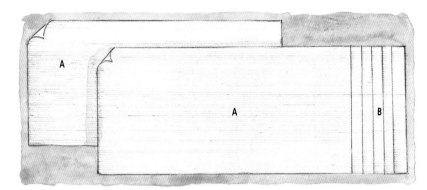

1 Using your measurements, mark the cutting lines on the grain of the fabric. Cut out the pieces.

2 To achieve the overall width of the main section, fabric widths will need to be joined. Cut one main cover piece (A) in half lengthways and place the two halves at either side of one full width. Pin and stitch the long seams. Press open.

3 Place the main cover centrally on the chair and, using card or a clean wooden spatula, tuck the fabric firmly into the chair at the back and sides of the seat and the back inside arms.

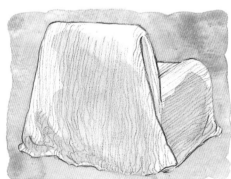

4 At the sides of the shoulders, arrange two or three 5cm (2in) pleats and smooth the folds down the sides of the chair.

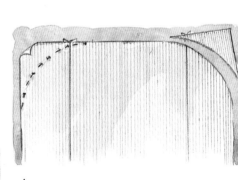

5 Similarly, arrange four or five 2.5cm (1in) pleats above the front arms and smooth the folds down the front of the chair.

6 Mark the lower edge, curving the corners and the front and back edges of the cover. Remove the cover and cut around to shape. Zigzag stitch to neaten the raw edges.

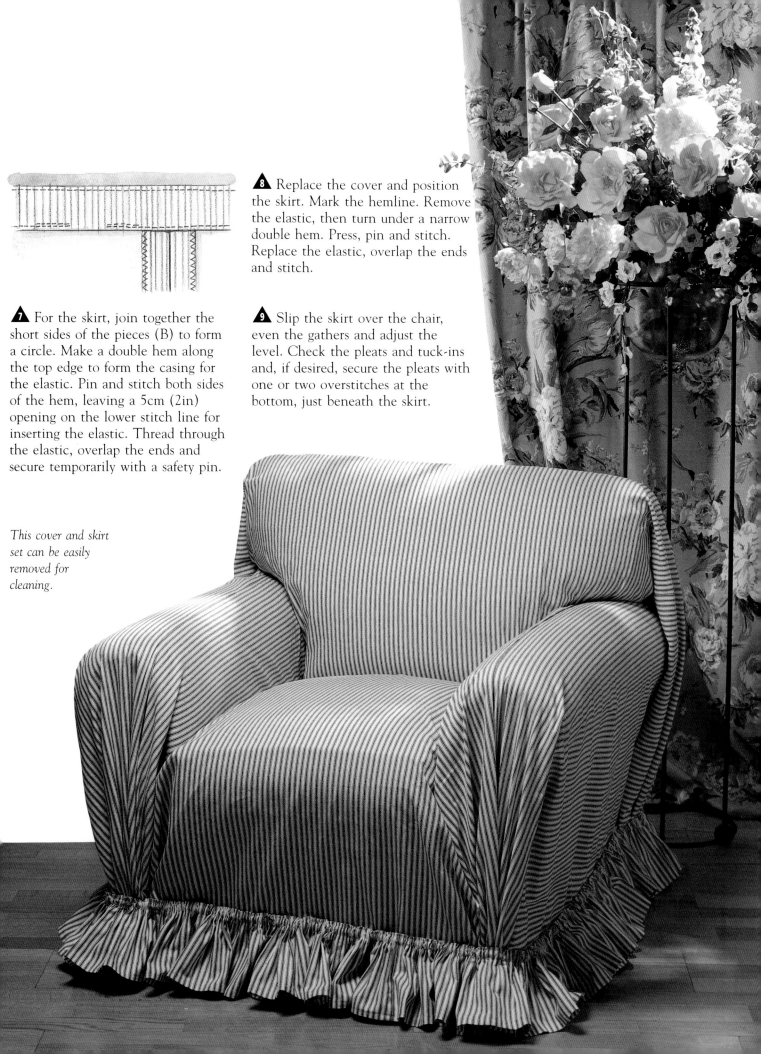

8 Replace the cover and position the skirt. Mark the hemline. Remove the elastic, then turn under a narrow double hem. Press, pin and stitch. Replace the elastic, overlap the ends and stitch.

7 For the skirt, join together the short sides of the pieces (B) to form a circle. Make a double hem along the top edge to form the casing for the elastic. Pin and stitch both sides of the hem, leaving a 5cm (2in) opening on the lower stitch line for inserting the elastic. Thread through the elastic, overlap the ends and secure temporarily with a safety pin.

9 Slip the skirt over the chair, even the gathers and adjust the level. Check the pleats and tuck-ins and, if desired, secure the pleats with one or two overstitches at the bottom, just beneath the skirt.

This cover and skirt set can be easily removed for cleaning.

WINTER WARMER

A simple cosy cover to throw over a chair when the cold weather sets in.

C H E C K L I S T

Materials

heavyweight furnishing fabric
iron-on fusible webbing
general sewing equipment   page 110–11

Techniques

machine stitching   page 114–15

Measuring up

Width – Measure from floor to floor on either side. Allow for tuck-ins at both inside arms and hem allowances.

Depth – Measure from floor level in front to floor in back. Allow for tuck-ins at the inside back and front of seat cushion; allow for deep pleats at front arms and hem allowances.

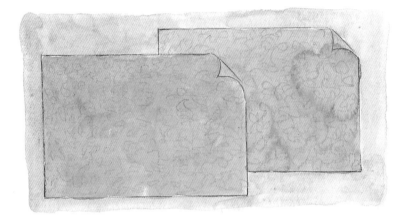

1 Using your measurements, mark the cutting line on the grain of the fabric, then cut out. If your fabric has a pattern, you may need to allow extra for matching.

2 Join the two lengths of fabric with a central seam.

3 Press the seam open. Neaten the long and short ends with double hems, either stitched or secured with iron-on fusible webbing.

4 With the seam of the fabric widthways to the chair, position the fabric so that there is more at the front to allow for pleating.

VARIATIONS

To keep this simple, we put the cushion under the cover but this treatment works just as well with the cushion on top. There will be more sewing and less tucking but the cushion will add to the tacking to help keep the pleats intact. You will need to allow for additional fabric. Instructions for box cushion covers are in the project on pages 78–9.

5 Depending on the size of your chair, place the fabric so that the seam falls either at the inside back or front edge of the seat. Begin tucking-in firmly along the inside back, checking the level of the fabric at the back. Adjust as necessary until the level of the back fabric is suitable.

6 Tuck-in the inside arms along the seat from back to front, pushing fabric down firmly. Use a clean wooden spatula to help push the fabric down.

8 Repeat step 6 for the other arm, pulling fabric as necessary and letting the pleats on the first arm fall if necessary. Arrange the pleats until there is only about 2.5cm (1in) trail on the floor in front. Secure with pins. Re-pleat the first arm to match the second and secure with pins. You may need to repeat steps 6 and 7 until the effect is suitable.

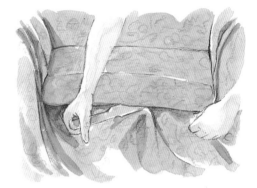

9 Tuck-in fabric under front seat cushion. Neaten the folds on the top and sides of the arms. Adjust as necessary.

7 Begin pleating one arm, starting with small pleats about 5cm (2in) deep, gradually getting larger until they double in size. Pleat until there is about 12.5cm (5in) of fabric trailing on the floor in front.

A large bedspread could also be used for this treatment; use something dark and heavy for winter and change to a light cotton spread in summer.

10 Secure the pleats with tacking stitches and remove the pins.

BOX PLEATED SKIRT

The fabric allowance (1.8m/2yds) for the following skirts is based on the size of an average armchair.

CHECKLIST

Materials

closely woven furnishing fabric
press fastener
pre-shrunk piping cord
general sewing equipment   page 110–11

Techniques

frills and pleats   page 120–21
piping and binding   page 118–19

Measuring up

To the following measurements, add 1.5cm (⅝in) for all seam allowances:
Skirt – Measure the perimeter at the base and allow three times this measurement for pleats, measure the depth plus hem allowance (A).
Bias strips – Measure the perimeter at the base and allow 4cm (1½in) for the width (B).

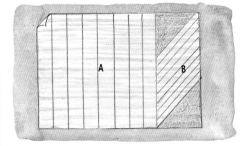

1 Using your measurements, mark the cutting lines on the grain of the fabric and cut out. Mark the letters on each piece.

2 Make up the piping. Pin and tack to the lower edge of the cover, with the seam allowance of the closure extending beyond piping.

3 Stitch the skirt sections together along the short edges to make a continuous length of fabric. Press seams open. Zigzag the top edge to neaten. Turn under a double hem on the lower edge.

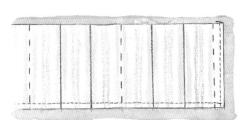

4 Determine the size of the pleats (ours are 7.5cm/3in wide) and mark up the fabric as shown, using chalk. Solid lines are fold lines; dotted lines are placement lines. Allow for a non-pleated overlap at one end, which will correspond with the opening facing on the cover.

5 Fold the box pleats, then tack along the top and bottom edges. Press on both sides of the fabric.

6 Tack the skirt to the cover, right sides together, with the piping between and the seam allowance of the cover opening extending. Stitch through all layers. Neaten the edges together and press the seam towards the cover.

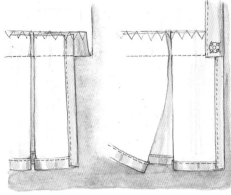

7 On the opening edge of the cover, neaten the hem folding it over the skirt seam to secure. Attach the press fastener.

FRILLED SKIRT

This skirt lends an informal, country-style touch to sofa and armchair covers.

CHECKLIST

Materials

closely woven furnishing fabric
hook-and-eye fastener
general sewing equipment   page 110–11

Techniques

making binding   page 118–19
frills and pleats   page 120–21

Measuring up

To the following measurements, add 1.5cm (⅝in) for seam allowances:
Skirt – Measure the perimeter at the base and add half the measurement for gathered fullness, and the depth plus hem allowance (A).
Bias strips – Measure the perimeter at the base and multiply by three, and allow 5cm (2in) for the width (B).

1 Using your measurements, mark the cutting lines on the grain of the fabric and cut out. Mark the letters on each piece.

2 Stitch the skirt together along the short sides to make a continuous length of fabric. Neaten the seams and press open. On the two outer edges, which will form the slipcover opening, turn under a double hem.

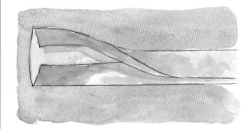

3 Join the bias strips along the short edges to make up the required length. With wrong sides together, fold the edges so they meet in the middle and press. Place the two folded edges together and press.

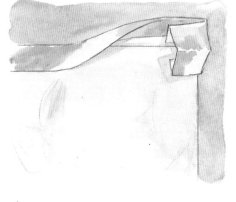

4 Pin the binding over both raw edges of the skirt, then tack and stitch in place from the right side (catching in the back). On the outside edges, fold the raw edges of the binding over the edge of the frill to neaten.

5 Run two rows of gathering stitches 4cm (1½in) from the top edge of the skirt. Pull up the threads, breaking the thread at regular intervals and wrapping around pins to secure, until the skirt fits the cover. Space the gathers evenly.

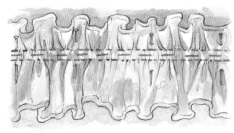

6 Tack to the cover between the gathering stitches. Stitch, then remove gathering threads. Attach a hook-and-eye to the opening edge.

LAYERED SKIRT

This skirt is most effective on long pieces of furniture, such as sofas or daybeds.

C H E C K L I S T

Materials

closely woven furnishing cotton – top skirt
silk or voile – underskirt
pre-shrunk piping cord
shank buttons and tassels
fabric adhesive
hook-and-eye fastener
standard curtain tape
general sewing equipment   page 110–11

Techniques

piping and binding   page 118–19
frills and pleats   page 120–21

Measuring up

To the following measurements, add 1.5cm (⅝in) for seam allowances:
Top skirt – Measure the perimeter at the base plus end hem allowances and the depth plus hem allowance (A).
Underskirt – Measure the perimeter at the base plus end hem allowance and add half the total measurement for gathered fullness, and the depth plus hem allowance (B).

SKIRT VARIATIONS

1 Using your measurements, mark the cutting lines on the grain of the fabric and cut out.

2 Stitch the top skirt together along the short sides to form a continuous length. Neaten the seams and press open. Turn under a double hem on the outer edges.

3 Calculate the number of points required on the long and short sides of your sofa or chair. Determine the width of each point, then mark the centre of each point using pins on the furniture and on the wrong side of the fabric. Divide the rectangles in half lengthways and mark a horizontal line 20cm (8in) from the top edge.

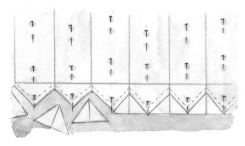

4 Using a ruler and pencil, draw in the points. Add a seam allowance and cut out.

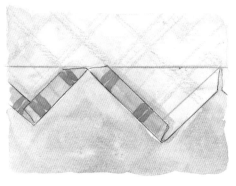

5 Snip into the inner angle of the points. Fold a single turning to the wrong side and press. Stitch or use fabric adhesive to secure the hem.

6 Stitch the underskirt as in step 2. On the top edge, fold a 2.5cm (1in) turning to the wrong side. Pin and stitch curtain tape below the folded edge.

7 Working from both ends, draw up the gathering cords so that the skirt fits around the chair or sofa. Knot the ends and even the gathers.

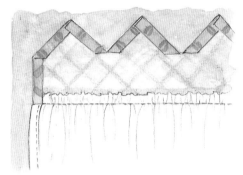

8 Place both skirts right sides together with the points of the top skirt facing upwards. Tack and stitch through all layers.

9 Attach the tassels to the points, stitching them through the looped end. To finish, cover each tassel end with a button, stitching it to the point through the shank.

To avoid sewing through many layers, skirts without piping can be attached to the cover with press fasteners. This has the extra advantage of making the skirt easily removable for washing or mending.

CHAIRS

The most basic upright chair can be given a completely new look with the right cover. The projects in this chapter encompass the full range of possibilities, from long gathered skirts with ties, to director's chairs. All are clearly explained and fully illustrated, so whatever your furnishing style, there is something for you.

BASIC CHAIR COVER

We've chosen a bold geometric pattern but this cover would look good in any fabric.

C H E C K L I S T

Materials

closely woven furnishing fabric
ribbon for ties
general sewing equipment   page 110–11

Techniques

mock pleats   page 120–21

Measuring up

To the following measurements, add 1.5cm (⅝in) for all seam allowances:
Outside and inside back – Measure the width and the depth from the inside edge of the seat to the seat level at the back (A).
Seat – Measure width and depth (B).
Skirts – Measure width and depth at both front and back, and sides plus hem allowance (C).
Mock pleats – Measure length and width: our width is 18cm (7in); allow four pieces (D).

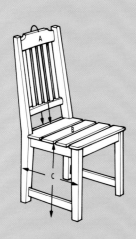

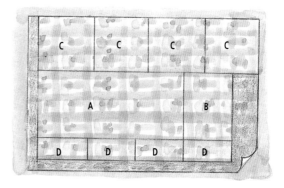

1 Using your measurments, mark the cutting lines on the grain of the fabric and cut out. Mark the letters on each piece.

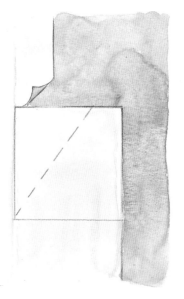

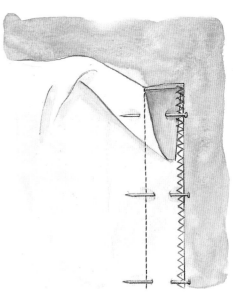

2 Fold the back section (A) in half widthways, right sides together. At each top corner, mark a square that corresponds to the thickness of the chair frame. On the outside back, trim away 1.5cm (⅝in) from the edges. Fold the square diagonally, then snip into outside back seam allowance.

3 Pin together the two side edges, folding down the dart, so the top edge runs parallel to the main seam. Stitch, then zigzag raw edges together. Repeat on the other side.

4 Put the back section on the chair wrong side out and position the seat fabric (B). Pin to the inside back right sides together, then tack.

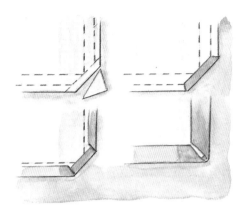

8 Cut eight lengths of ribbon, ours measure 25cm (10in). Turn under one end. Handstitch it behind the hemmed edges on each corner. Trim the loose ribbon ends diagonally. Tie into bows to secure the cover.

This versatile style can be used on a chair for any room in the house.

5 On the skirt (C) and mock pleat (D) pieces, trim away just the tips of the bottom corners. Make narrow double hems by first turning under the corner, then the sides, and the sides again forming mitred corners. Pin, tack and stitch.

6 Replace the cover wrong side out. Pin the skirt sections (C) to the seat section so that the edges meet evenly at the front and back corners. Position pleat sections (D) centrally over each front corner. Pin, tack and stitch through all layers. Trim and neaten the raw edges.

7 Turn right side out and place on chair to check fit. Mark the position of the corner ties about 6cm (2½in) down from the seat edge.

FULL-LENGTH COVER

This sophisticated cover was designed for a chair with a padded seat.

CHECKLIST

Materials

closely woven furnishing fabric
pre-shrunk piping cord
general sewing equipment   page 110–11

Techniques

piping and binding   page 118–19
frills and pleats   page 120–21

Measuring up

To the following measurements, add 1.5cm (⅝in) seam allowances:

Inside back – Measure the width plus the width of the struts and depth (A).

Outside back – Measure the width and depth to the seat (B).

Seat – Measure the width and depth (C).

Seat gusset – Measure the length from one back strut to the other and depth (D).

Skirt – Measure the depth and allow 1½ times the perimeter for the gather (E).

Ties – Allow eight pairs of ties, ours are 30 × 7cm (12 × 2¾in) (F).

Facings – Measure the width of the struts and the depth from top of chair to inside back seat edge (G).

Piping – Allow for bias strips (H).

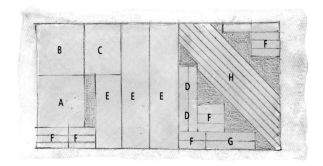

1 Using your measurements, mark the cutting lines on the grain of the fabric and cut out. Mark the letters on the pieces.

2 Make up enough piping for: the chair back, the gusset top and bottom and the top of the back skirt.

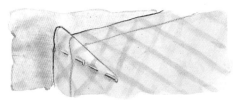

3 Place the inside back (A) on the chair, wrong side out. Mark the seamlines. Pin a dart across the top corners at right angles to the chair sides to accommodate the thickness.

4 Right sides together, pin and stitch the inside back to the seat (C); let the excess extend on each side. Mark the seat seamline, curve front corners to fit, then trim.

5 Tack piping around the sides and front of the seat, right sides together, extending to cover the fabric allowance at each side of the inside back.

6 Right sides together, pin and stitch the gusset (D) to the seat over the piping. Trim and neaten seams.

7 With the cover on the chair, mark the tie positions at four evenly spaced intervals. For each tie, fold the fabric in half lengthways, right sides together. Pin and stitch the long edges and one short edge. Trim, turn right side out and press.

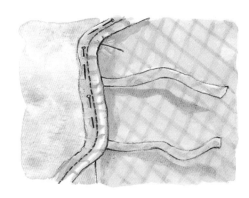

8 Pin and tack ties in position. Pin and tack piping around the inside back and lower edge of the gusset in one continuous strip.

9 Mark the seamline on the outside back (B), rounding the corners to fit the chair. Pipe the lower edge and neaten the piping ends. Tack the ties as marked.

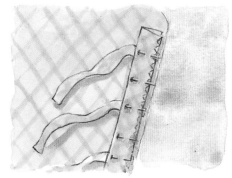

10 Make up facings to neaten the back edges of the side openings, which should end level with the last tie. Fold the fabric sections (G) in half lengthways and pin to each side, right sides together. Stitch, catching the ties.

11 Pin and tack the outside back to the inside back, right sides together. Stitch along the top edge only, using the zipper foot and stitching close to the piping.

12 The skirt is made in two parts: the back (the width from back leg to back leg) and the front (from one back leg around the front to the other back leg). Join the skirt pieces (E) for the front skirt along the short edges. Hem the side openings and bottom edge. Stitch two rows of gathering threads along the top edge. Pull up the gathers evenly to fit the lower edge of the gusset.

13 Pin the main skirt to the lower edge of the gusset with the right sides together, then stitch around through all layers. Trim and neaten the raw edges. Repeat on the back section, making sure the edges of the skirt are equal at the side opening.

14 Turn the cover right side out and fit it over the chair, fastening the ties into bows.

A set of these chair covers looks stunning around a dining room table.

TWO-PIECE CHAIR COVER

This cover is designed for upright chairs with upholstered seats.

C H E C K L I S T

Materials

closely woven furnishing fabric
medium-weight synthetic wadding
paper for pattern
general sewing equipment   page 110–11

Techniques

piping and binding   page 118–19
using wadding   page 122–25

Measuring up

To the following measurements, add 1.5cm (⅝in) seam allowances:
Inside and outside back – Measure length and width; allow two pieces (A).
Seat cover – Measure the width and depth; allow two pieces (B). Make a paper pattern for the shape, see step 2.
Binding – Allow enough fabric for the perimeter of the back and seat covers, with a depth of about 5cm (2in) (C).
Ties – Allow for ten pairs of ties (D), ours measure 5cm (2in) wide and 25.5cm (10in) long.

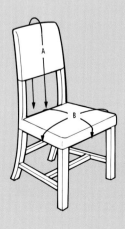

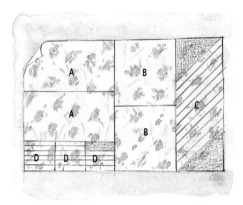

1 Using your measurements, mark the cutting lines on the grain of the fabric and cut out. Mark the letters on each piece

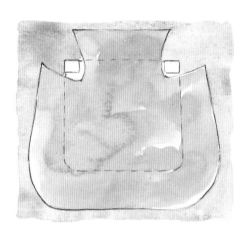

2 Lay paper over the seat, extending down over the upholstery. Mark all around, allowing for the back struts. Mark seam allowances. Cut out and round front corners.

3 Using your measurements for the chair back, make a paper pattern. Round the corners, then mark seam allowances and cut out.

4 Place the patterns on the fabric sections and cut out. From the wadding, cut one back and one seat piece along the seam allowances.

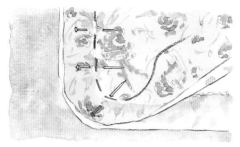

5 Place the two back pieces wrong sides together. Slide the wadding in between, then pin and tack.

6 Make six ties for the chair back. Fold each piece of fabric in half lengthways, right sides together. Pin, then stitch the long side and one short side, with a 1cm (⅜in) seam allowance. Trim, turn right side out and press.

7 To mark the position of the ties, place the back piece on the chair. Mark the first set about 5cm (2in) up from the lower edge and space the other two evenly between this set and the centre fold. Pin and tack the ties to the underside, matching the raw edges of the ties to those of the back piece.

8 Join the binding pieces to form two long strips: one for the seat and one for the back.

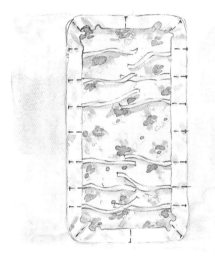

9 Pin the back binding around the edge, right sides together and over the ties. Stitch, taking a 1cm (⅜in) seam allowance. Turn under the binding, then fold over the raw edge to the right side. Pin and stitch through all layers.

10 Make up four pairs of seat ties as in step 6. On one seat section, pin and tack two pairs on both sides of the back strut shaping. Pin both seat pieces right sides together and stitch around the back shaping. Clip into the curved seam allowances, turn right side out and press.

11 Insert the wadding as in step 5.

12 Cover the raw edges of the main seat section with the binding, as in step 9.

13 Place the cover on the seat. Holding it firmly in position, fold the front edges into a large dart at each corner. Mark the points where the fabric meets for the ties.

14 Handstitch the seat ties on the underside, as marked, positioning them parallel with the outside edges. When these are tied behind the chair legs, they will hold the cover in position.

We used the same fabric on both sides but you could also use different fabrics for reversible covers.

SEAT CUSHION WITH BOW

Flower and check prints complement one another in this cheery chair cover.

CHECKLIST

Materials

closely woven furnishing fabric
medium-weight synthetic wadding
paper for pattern
general sewing equipment   page 110–11

Techniques

using wadding   page 122–25

Measuring up

To the following measurements, add 1.5cm (⅝in) seam allowances:
Seat (fabric and wadding) – Measure width and depth (A). Make a paper pattern for the shape, see step 2.
Gusset – Measure perimeter of chair seat and depth (B).
Front skirt – Measure width and multiply depth by two (C).
Side skirts – Measure width and multiply depth by two (D).
NOTE: Skirts are double thickness.
Ties – Allow four pieces, ours measure 71 × 10cm (28 × 4in) each (E).

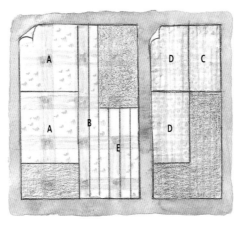

1 Using your measurements, mark the cutting lines on the grain of the fabric and cut out. Mark the letters on each piece.

2 Lay paper over the seat and mark around the outside edges and along the back edge, marking inside the struts. Add the seam allowance and cut out.

3 Place the pattern on the seat fabric sections (A) and cut out. Repeat for the wadding. On the seat, gusset (B) and front skirt (C) mark the centre front, and centre back where appropriate.

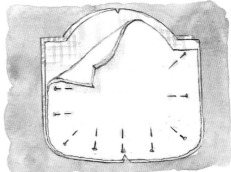

4 Place the two seat pieces with right sides together. Pin the wadding to one piece. On the back edge, trim the wadding just clear of the seam allowance. Pin and stitch across the back edge between the corners. Trim, snip into the curved seam and turn right side out. Tack the remaining edges together.

5 Place the tie pieces with the right sides together in pairs. Pin and stitch around, stitching diagonally across one short end and leaving the remaining short end open. Snip across the corners of the seam allowance, trim and turn right side out. Press the seams. Pleat the raw edges to fit the width of the gusset and tack to secure. Position each tie piece at the ends of the gusset pieces, laying the ties on the gussets, right sides together and raw edges matching. Pin and tack.

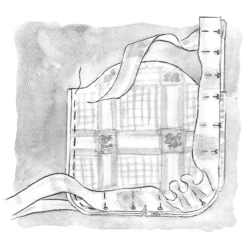

6 Place the gussets with the right sides together and the ties inside. With the centre fronts matching, slide the seat between the gusset pieces towards the lower edge of the gusset (the top edge when turned

right side out). Pin and stitch across the gusset ends, catching in the ties. Continue, stitching the gusset only, then around the top edge of the gusset also catching in the seat and stitching through all layers. Trim, turn right side out and press. Tack the remaining raw edges of the gussets together.

7 Fold the front skirt (C) in half, right sides together; pin and stitch the side edges only. Trim and turn right side out. Tack the top raw edges together. Repeat for the side skirt pieces (D). Press the seams.

8 Place the skirt pieces on the right side of the gusset, with raw edges matching and the front corners of the skirt evenly positioned. Pin and stitch to the combined gusset edges. Trim and neaten the raw edges together. Place the cover over the seat and form the ties into a bow at the back.

Depending on your chair, you may need to attach touch-and-close fastening to the ties and seat back to keep the bow in place.

PLEATED SKIRT COVER

Buttons add interest to this
classic cover.

CHECKLIST

Materials

closely woven furnishing fabric
medum-weight synthetic wadding
paper for patterns
two decorative buttons
general sewing equipment   page 110–11

Techniques

box pleats   page 120–21
using wadding   page 122–25

Measuring up

To each of the following measurements, add
1.5cm ($\frac{5}{8}$in) seam allowances:
Main seat (fabric and wadding) – Measure
width and depth to struts and allow for two
pieces (A), make a paper pattern for the
shape, see step 2.
Gusset – Measure the perimeter of the seat
and depth; allow for double thickness (B).
Skirt – Allow three times the perimeter and
depth plus the hem allowance (C).
Seat outside back – Measure length and
depth of seat behind struts (D).
Button loops – Allow two small rectangular
fabric pieces.

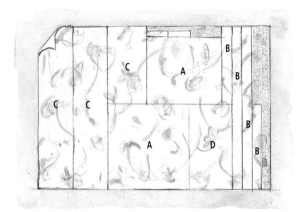

1 Using your measurements, mark
the cutting lines on the grain of the
fabric and cut out. Mark the letters
on the pieces.

2 Lay a sheet of paper on the seat
and mark the contours with pencil.
Add the seam allowance, then cut
out the pattern. Repeat to make a
pattern for the seat outside back.
Mark the button and loop positions
as shown.

3 Cut out the seat (A) and seat
outside back (D) to shape. Repeat
for the wadding (seat only).

4 Stitch together the short edges
of the skirt pieces (C). Press the
seams to one side, then neaten raw
edges. Turn under a double hem.

5 Fold the skirt fabric into 8cm
($3\frac{1}{4}$in) box pleats. Adjust the pleats
to fit the chair, making sure they fall
evenly at the front corners. Pin and
tack along the top edge to secure.

6 For the button loops, fold each
piece of fabric in half lengthways.
Pin and stitch the long edges. Trim
and turn right side out.

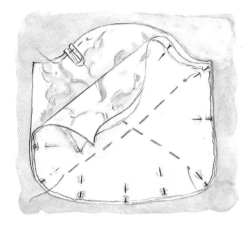

7 Fold each piece into a loop. Pin and tack in place as marked on main seat fabric. Place the main seat pieces, right sides together, with the wadding on top. Trim wadding clear of back seam allowance, then tack to one seat section. Pin and stitch back edge, then trim and turn right side out. Pin unsewn edges together.

8 Pin and stitch the outside seat sections (D) as in step 7, but leave the back edge open and do not use wadding. Trim, turn right side out and pin the back edges together.

9 To keep seams neat, the gusset is made from double thickness fabric. With right sides inside, pin and tack enough gusset pieces (B) together to form a circle. Put on chair to check for a snug fit. Repeat for the second (inner) gusset, then stitch.

10 With right sides together and centres matching, mark the centre front and centre back of one of the gusset pieces.

11 Pin one gusset to the seat and outside seat sections; allow space for the struts. Pin and tack all around. Right sides together, pin and stitch the second gusset to the underside of the seat and outside seat. Trim and turn right side out. Tack the remaining gusset edges together.

12 Right sides together, pin the top of the skirt to the gusset. Place so that a fold falls on front corners. Tack, stitch, then zigzag raw edges.

13 Sew on the buttons to correspond with the loops.

Increase the cost-saving benefits of home-sewing by making the bottom seat and gusset pieces from calico.

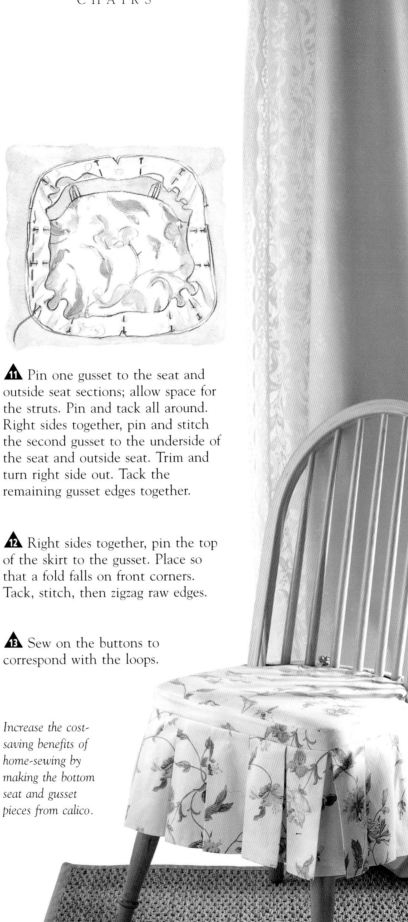

FOLDING CHAIR COVER

Give your folding chairs a designer look for summer with this stylish, easy-going cover.

CHECKLIST

Materials

heavyweight cotton furnishing fabric
paper for pattern
general sewing equipment   page 110–11

Techniques

patterned fabric   page 122–25
inverted pleats   page 120–21

Measuring up

To the following measurements, add 1.5cm (⅝in) seam allowances:

Seat – Measure width and depth (A), plus 2.5cm (1in) for ease. Make a paper pattern for the shape, see step 2.

Inside back – Measure width and the depth to the seat (B).

Outside back – Measure the width around the back legs and depth from top of inside back to floor (C) plus hem allowance.

Front skirt – Measure the top width around three sides of the seat plus 30cm (12in) for inverted pleats, and depth plus hem allowance (D).

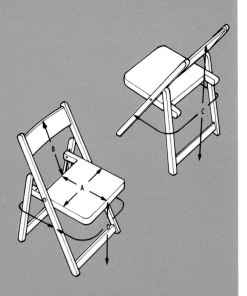

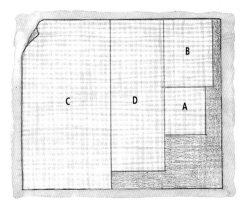

1 Using your measurements, mark the cutting lines on the grain of the fabric and cut out. Mark the letters on each piece.

2 For the shaped seat section, lay paper on the seat and trace around the edges, curving along the inside back edge. Cut out the seat piece (A) using the paper pattern.

3 With a check, you will need to adjust the fabric to ensure that the centre line of every piece matches. On the appropriate pieces (back pieces, seat and skirt), notch the seam allowance to mark centre points.

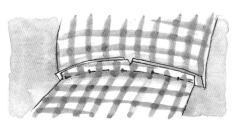

4 Lay the seat (A) and inside back (B) on the chair, wrong sides out. Pin where they meet along the curved line of the inside back edge, matching centre notches. Tack, then stitch. Press the seam towards the back.

5 Place on the chair, wrong side out. Pin the outside back (C) to the inside back (B) along the top, matching centre notches. Following the angle of the chair frame, pin the back and front together at the sides, as far as the seat. The seamline at the top is taken along the top edge of the inside back, so you will need small darts at the top corners of the outside back to allow for the struts.

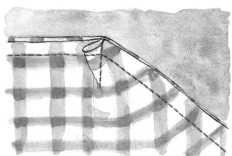

6 Tack and stitch the darts, then trim the seams as far as the seat. Place on the chair wrong side out and pin around the back.

7 Pin on the skirt (D), matching centre notches. Fold the front corners into 7.5cm (3in) deep pleats. Pin, then tack.

8 Pin the skirt where it meets the other pieces at the seat back; allow for the width of the strut. Tack and stitch all around the seat. Press.

9 With wrong sides out, pin the diagonal seamlines so that the fabric hangs smoothly from the seat to the floor and the back to the floor remains at right angles.

10 Remove and trim excess fabric. Stitch and press. Place on the chair and mark the hemline. Turn under, return to the chair to check fit, then pin and stitch.

With such an elegant cover, your folding chairs can be brought to the dining table. Make one set of covers for everyday use and another set for entertaining.

DIRECTOR'S CHAIR COVER

In a child's room or in the garden, this all-season denim cover will transform an ordinary director's chair.

CHECKLIST

Materials

hard-wearing denim
fabric adhesive
general sewing equipment   page 110–11

Techniques

machine stitching   page 114–15

Measuring up

To the following measurements, add 1.5cm (⅝in) seam allowances:

Inside back – Measure width and depth from inside back edge over the top allowing for the width of the struts (A).

Outside back – Measure width and depth to floor (B).

Seat – Measure width and depth, allowing 2.5cm (1in) for all around ease (C).

Arms – Measure width and depth from seat over the arm and down to the floor (D).

Front skirt – Measure width and depth (E).

Bows – Allow two squares, ours measure 25.5cm (10in), plus two rectangular strips (F).

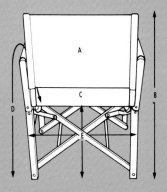

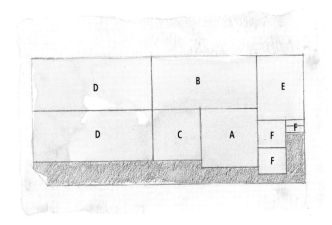

1 Using your measurements, mark the cutting lines on the grain of fabric and cut out. Mark the letters on each piece and neaten raw edges.

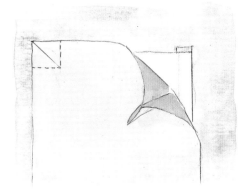

2 On the inside back (A), form darts at the top corners to accommodate the width of the chair struts. Fold the darts, right sides together. Tack and machine stitch. Remove the tacking and trim excess.

3 Place the inside back on the chair. Mark the points where the arm rests break into the vertical line, then cut out a narrow rectangle, as shown, to accommodate them.

4 To allow for the canvas chair back bowing when under pressure, add two darts just in from the lower inside back corners. Pin and stitch. Trim and press the seam towards the inside back.

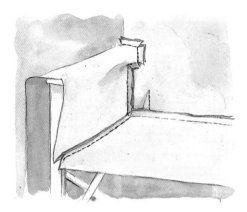

5 Place the inside back and the seat (C) on the chair, wrong sides out and pin and stitch. Trim seam allowances. Pin the arm pieces (D) to the seat sides. Mark, then cut out a rectangle from front edge of arm to match that on the inside back. Stitch the seat to the arms on both sides, then to the inside back, stitching between the rectangles.

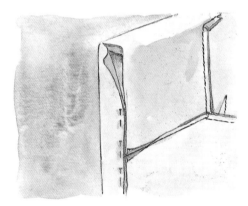

6 Bring the outside arm pieces across to meet the front edge of the inside arms. Pin, tack and stitch, curving the angled seam over the front arm rests.

7 With right sides together, pin the outside and inside back together along the top and down the sides, as far as the arm rests. Ease the outside back around the arm rest and continue to pin together the outside back and outside arm pieces. Remove, tack and stitch.

8 Replace the cover, wrong side out and pin the front skirt (E) to the seat and the outside arm pieces. Tack and stitch.

9 Replace the cover and mark the hemline. Turn under a double hem.

10 Neaten the edges on the bow pieces (F) with narrow turnings. Fold in the long edges of the bow strips (F) and glue. Pleat the bows like a fan, place a strip around the middle and stitch to the cover.

As the spirit takes you, your director's chair can be dressed for the part. Here in rugged denim with bows, but diaphanous muslin with dried flowers could be next.

DECK CHAIR

Covering your outdoor furniture is simple and requires a minimum of sewing.

C H E C K L I S T

Materials

heavyweight deck chair canvas
heavy-duty sewing machine needle and thread
heavy-duty staples and staple gun (or hammer, drawing pins and upholstery nails)
set square and ruler
general sewing equipment   page 110–11

Techniques

machine stitching   page 114–15

Measuring up

Measure the width between the struts at the bottom and the top. Lay the chair flat and measure the length, allowing extra to wrap around the top rail for securing the canvas.

1 If your canvas is only slightly wider than the chair frame, turn under a single hem on both long edges to fit.

2 Using the set square and ruler, check that both ends of the canvas form true right angles. Trim to adjust if necessary. Zigzag short edges to prevent fraying.

3 Position the top edge of the canvas on the underside of the top fixing strut, with the canvas parallel to the edge of the strut. Working outwards from the middle, insert evenly spaced staples.

4 Alternatively, to nail the canvas in place, position it in the same way as before. Hold in place temporarily with one or two drawing pins, then secure with evenly spaced upholstery nails.

5 Wrap the canvas once around the top strut, smoothing it evenly. Turn the frame over and, pulling the canvas taut, take it around the bottom strut. Staple or nail in position as before.

Bright, floral striped fabric will perk up any patio.

STAPLES AND NAILS

A staple gun is useful for attaching fabric quickly and effectively to a wooden frame. Warning: always point the gun away from you as the staples can be fired accidentally.

Upholsterer's tacks (nails) come in two varieties: improved tacks which have large heads and fine tacks with smaller heads. Use with an ordinary woodworking or upholsterer's hammer, which has a comparatively heavier head, to tap in the tacks firmly.

Either of these techniques can also be used for permanently attaching fabric to a stool top or chair seat, for example. You can cover the staples or tacks with silk braid or fringed edging, glued with fabric adhesive.

CAPTAIN'S CHAIR

Make two different canvas slings for your chair and you can change them with the seasons.

CHECKLIST

Materials

heavyweight deck chair canvas
heavy-duty sewing machine needle and thread
set square and ruler
nylon cord
heavy-duty eyelet kit
general sewing equipment   page 110–11

Techniques

machine stitching   page 114–15

Measuring up

Allow one length of fabric. Measure the width between the struts top and bottom; add 5cm (2in) for hem allowances. Measure the length of the back and seat and allow double fabric; add 50cm (20in) for deep hems at the short edges.

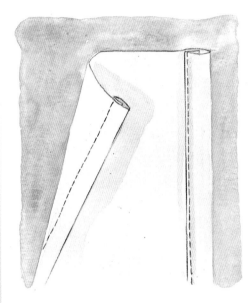

1 With the wrong side facing, make narrow double turnings along both long edges and stitch.

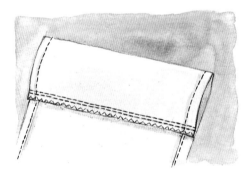

2 Make sure the corners of the two short sides are at right angles to the long sides: trim, if necessary, and zigzag to neaten. On both short sides, turn under a deep, 13cm (5in) hem to the wrong side. Pin and stitch across the neatened edge with a 12mm (½in) seam. Stitch a second row just inside of the first stitch line.

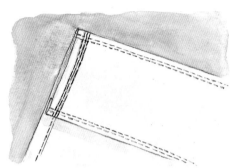

3 Stitch across the folded edge of each end, 2.5cm (1in) inside the fold. Depending on your fabric, stitch a second line 6mm (¼in) inside the first one, for added strength.

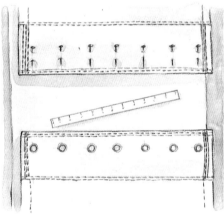

4 On both short sides, mark the position of the seven eyelets evenly outside the double stitchline on the folded edge. Follow the instructions given with the kit to insert the heavy-duty eyelets.

5 Place the cover on the chair, taking it from the top, under the lower back strut, over the front seat rail and back under the lower back strut, so the short ends meet at the outside back.

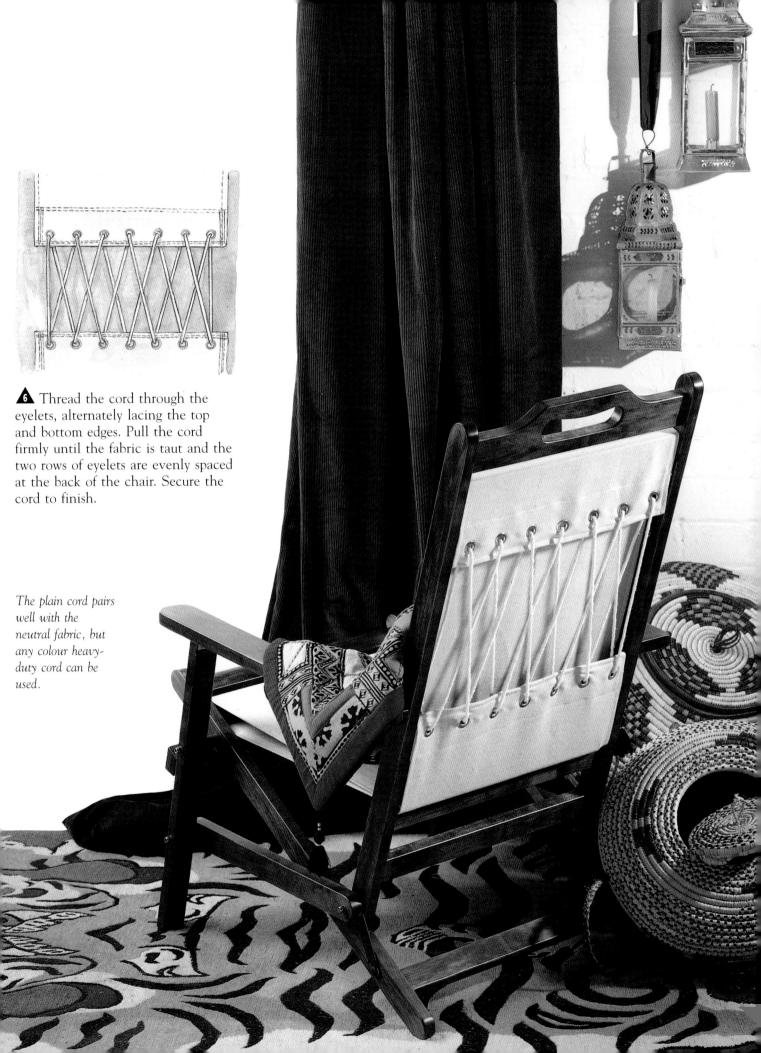

6 Thread the cord through the eyelets, alternately lacing the top and bottom edges. Pull the cord firmly until the fabric is taut and the two rows of eyelets are evenly spaced at the back of the chair. Secure the cord to finish.

The plain cord pairs well with the neutral fabric, but any colour heavy-duty cord can be used.

DIRECTOR'S CHAIR

FIXED COVERS

Replacing worn covers will extend the life of these fold-up chairs – useful for extra seating inside or outside the home.

C H E C K L I S T

Materials

heavyweight deck chair canvas
heavy-duty sewing machine needle and thread
heavy-duty staples and staple gun or hammer and upholstery nails
set square and ruler
large eyelet kit
general sewing equipment   page 110–11

Techniques

machine stitching   page 114–15

Measuring up

Seat – Measure the width plus 18cm (7in) for hem allowances and wrap around. Measure the depth plus 8cm (3in) for hem allowances **(A)**.
Back – Measure the width plus 18cm (7in) for hems and wrap around. Measure the depth from within the curve of the batten, plus 8cm (3in) for hem allowances **(B)**.

1 Using the old cover as a template or your measurements, mark the cutting lines horizontally on the straight grain of the fabric. If using fabric with a pattern, it should run vertically. Cut out the pieces.

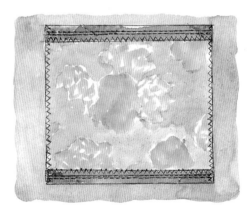

2 On the seat section, zigzag all four raw edges to neaten. Turn under a single 2.5cm (1in) hem to the wrong side along the front and back edges and stitch across. Stitch a second line 6mm (¼in) inside the previous stitching.

3 Along each side edge of the seat section, turn under and press single 2.5cm (1in) turnings to the wrong side of the fabric.

4 Lay the chair on its side and position the side edge of the fabric centrally on the inner underside edge of the seat frame, attaching with only a few staples to check fit. The pressed edge should run parallel with the underside edge of the frame.

5 Working outwards from the centre of the chair, nail or staple the seat section in place to the underside of the frame.

6 Turn the chair to the opposite side. In the same way, attach the seat first with two or three staples. Check the fit and adjust if necessary, before nailing or stapling the second side in place.

7 On the back piece, zigzag the raw edges along the top and lower edges. Turn under a single 2.5cm (1in) hem on each edge and stitch in place with two rows of stitching as before.

8 Zigzag stitch the two side edges. Turn under the side edges with single 2.5cm (1in) hems and press.

9 To mark the position of the bolt holes on the fabric, wrap the side edges of the fabric around the battens (they will already have been removed from the chair). You will need two holes on either side of the battens. Check that the chair back fits the chair, then working from the wrong side, fix the eyelets in place.

11 Replace the chair back so that the battens are behind the fabric at the back.

10 Position the fabric edges, right side against the wood, along the rear inside edge of the wooden battens. Working outwards from the middle, staple or nail the fabric to the batten, making sure the eyelets align with the holes in the chair frame.

A new cover will not look as good on an old frame so be sure to sand and paint or varnish your chair before fixing the fabric.

MEASURING UP
Instead of measuring, make use of the old cover. Remove the worn cover from the chair and, as you do, make a note of how the individual pieces have been attached. Open out the fabric pieces, unpick any seams and press them flat. Use these to estimate the quantities required for the new cover and, if they are in good shape, save them to be used as pattern pieces. Do not use if the old cover is stretched.

BEDROOMS & BOUDOIRS

Rooms to relax in require
adaptable covers and the
projects in this chapter are just that,
whether your style is formal, rustic
or modern. From the clean, classical
lines of a daybed with bolster
cushions, to a futon with a
contemporary look, these covers
are designed to look good, night
and day.

DAYBED COVER

Bolster cushions and a skirt
add elegance to a daybed.

CHECKLIST

Materials

closely woven furnishing fabric
pre-shrunk piping cord
zip for the box cushion: 15cm (6in)
   longer than the back edge
zips for bolsters: 15cm (6in) shorter
   than the length
general sewing equipment   page 110–11

Techniques

piping and binding   page 118–19
inserting zips   page 116–17
inverted pleats   page 120–21

Measuring up

To the following measurements, add 1.5cm
(⅝in) seam allowances:
Box cushion – Measure length and width (A);
allow for top and bottom pieces.
Front cushion gusset – Measure length from
mid-sides and depth (B).
Back cushion gusset – Measure length as for
B, and depth plus 3cm (1¼in) zip seam
allowance (C).
Skirt base (top panel) – Same as A (D).
Skirt – Measure width from mid-front to
mid-side plus 40cm (16in) per pleat, and
depth plus hem allowance (E).
Bolsters – Measure the circumference and
width of the main section (F); for the ends,
measure circumference plus the radius (G).
Piping – Allow for bias strips (H).

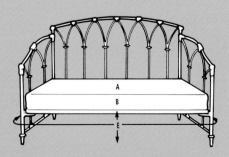

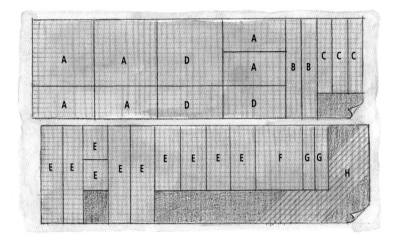

1 Using your measurements, mark
the cutting lines on the grain of the
fabric and cut out. Mark the letters
on each piece.

2 Make up sufficient piping to trim
the top and bottom edges of the
cushion and the bolsters.

3 To make up the box cushion
length, cut one fabric section A in
half widthways. Join the halves to
one full section along the short
edges, matching any pattern. Repeat
for the second cushion side.

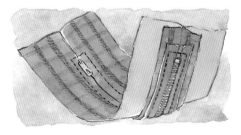

4 For the cushion zip, cut the back
gusset (C) in half lengthways. With
right sides together, tack and press
the seam open. Place the zip right
side down centrally over the wrong
side of the opening. Tack, then
stitch on the right side using the
zipper foot.

5 Stitch the gusset pieces (B and
C) along the short edges, leaving
1.5cm (⅝in) unstitched at each end
of the seams.

6 Tack piping around the top and
bottom edges of the cushion (A).
With right sides inside and front
corners matching, pin and stitch the
gusset to the top piece on all four
sides. Attach the cushion underside
in the same way.

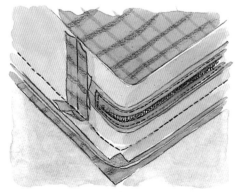

7 Snip into the seam allowances at
the corners, neaten the seams and
press. Remove tacking, open the zip
and turn right side out.

8 To make up the skirt, stitch the pieces (E) along the short edges and press the seams open. Turn under a double hem along the bottom edge.

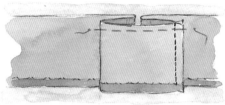

9 Arrange the skirt pleats, placing one at each corner and one centrally at each side. Tack across the top to hold. Press on both sides.

10 Place the top panel (D) and skirt right sides together, raw edges and corners matching. Tack, snip into corners at the seam allowance and stitch. Neaten the seams.

11 With right sides together, apply piping to the two short edges of the bolster sections (F).

12 To fit the bolster zip, fold the main section (F) in half widthways, right sides together. Tack across the ends, leaving a central opening the length of the zip. Stitch, then press open. Tack and stitch the zip in place, see step 4.

13 On one end piece (G), zigzag the long sides. Stitch the short sides, right sides together, and press the seam open. Repeat for the second end piece. Run two rows of gathering stitches along one turned under edge of each piece.

14 With right sides together, stitch the ends (G) to the main bolster sections.

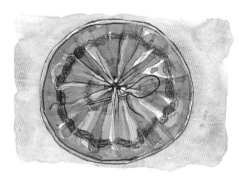

15 Pull up the gathers, bringing the edges together to form a circle. Fasten off securely. Attach tassels to the centre of each end, stitching the cord neatly behind the gathers.

To save time and money, skip the back skirt if your daybed is against a wall and make the skirt base panel from curtain lining or sheets.

HEADBOARD COVER

Coordinate your bedroom
furnishings with a fitted cover
for your bedhead, tied in place
with pretty bows.

CHECKLIST

Materials

closely woven furnishing cotton
paper for pattern
general sewing equipment   page 110–11

Techniques

machine stitching   page 114–15

Measuring up

To the following measurements, add 1.5cm
(⅝in) for all seam allowances:
Main panels – Measure width and depth (A),
then make a paper pattern for the shape, see
step 2.
Gusset – Measure the depth and length and
add 8cm (3in) at each end for a tuck-in (B).
Ties – Allow four pairs, ours measure each
25cm (10in) long by 3cm (1¼in) wide (C).

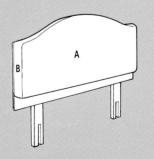

1 Using your measurements, mark
the cutting lines on the grain of the
fabric and cut out. Mark the letters
on each piece.

2 Pin paper to the headboard and
draw around the contour. Add 4cm
(1½in) to each side edge for hems
and 18cm (7in) to the bottom edge,
for a tuck-in and hem. Cut out one
fabric section to shape for the back.

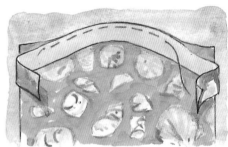

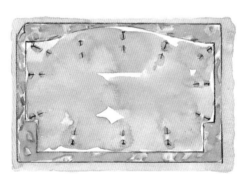

3 For the front panel, cut out the
lower corners on the paper pattern as
shown to allow for mitred corners
around the padding, then cut out the
fabric to shape.

4 With right sides together, pin
the gusset to the front panel, leaving
the outer 4cm (1½in) at either side
unstitched. Tack and stitch. Repeat
for the back panel. Press the seams
towards the gusset.

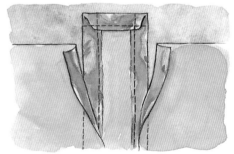

5 Stitch a double turning on the
short edges of the gusset. Neaten the
seam allowances by stitching a single
turning and folding in the corners
diagonally for mitred corners.

6 Turn under and stitch a double hem along the side edges of the front and back panels and along the bottom edges.

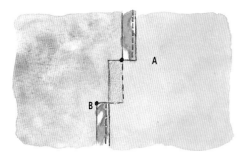

7 On the front panel, neaten the side edges as far as the cut-in and then neaten the tuck-in edge below, snipping across the seam allowance at point B. Trim away the shaded area, place points A and B together, right sides inside and stitch to form a mitred corner to accommodate the depth of the headboard.

8 For the ties, fold each piece so the raw edges of the long sides meet in the middle, wrong sides inside. Fold in half lengthways, then stitch. Alternatively, secure the cover using fabric loops and buttons, or simplify the task by using ribbons in place of the fabric ties.

If your bed is against a wall, use sheeting to make up the back side of the cover, which will cut down on the amount of furnishing fabric required.

9 Place the cover on the headboard right side out. Position the ties about 2cm (¾in) in from the edge. Fold in the ends, then tack and stitch.

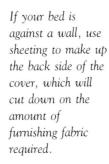

DRESSING TABLE COVER

Pretty fabrics, combined with elementary sewing skills, can be used imaginatively to dress up a dressing table.

CHECKLIST

Materials

three coordinating cotton furnishing fabrics
standard curtain heading tape and hooks
paper for pattern
fabric adhesive
general sewing equipment   page 110–11

Techniques

patterned fabric	page 122–25
frills and pleats	page 120–21
bias strips	page 118–19

Measuring up

To the following measurements, add 1.5cm (⅝in) for all seam allowances:
Table top – Measure length and width (A) and make a paper pattern for the shape, see step 2.
Scalloped band – Measure the perimeter and the depth plus hem allowance (B).
Skirt – Measure the perimeter and allow double for gathered fullness on the bias, and the depth (C).
Frill – For the width, double the perimeter measurement of the skirt, and measure the depth plus hem allowance (D).

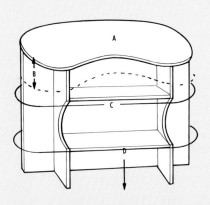

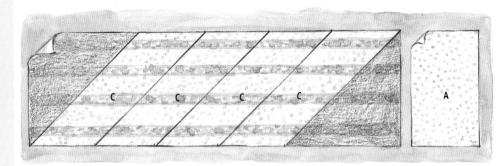

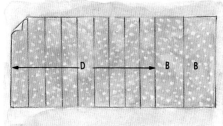

1 Using your measurements, mark the cutting lines for each section on the grain of the fabric and cut out. Mark the letters on each piece.

2 Lay paper over the dressing table top. Mark around the edge, add the seam allowance and cut out. Place the pattern on the table top fabric (A) and cut out.

3 To scallop the edge of the band, lay the fabric section B right side down. Divide evenly into desired scallop widths, then draw in the arcs, using a makeshift compass – a piece of string attached to tailor's chalk. An average scallop is 25cm (10in) wide by 5cm (2in) deep. Mark the seam allowance and hem and cut out. Snip into the seam allowance at the top of each scallop.

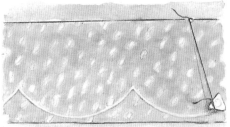

4 Following the hem mark, fold under a single turning and press. Work outwards from the middle of each scallop, creating small tucks in the hem where necessary. Secure with fabric adhesive and leave to dry. Alternatively, stitch the hem.

5 With right sides together, stitch the short edges of the band (B) to form a circle and press the seam open. Pin the table top to the band with the seam at the back. Tack and check fit before stitching. Press the seam towards the band.

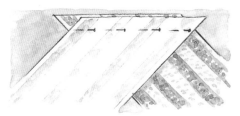

6 Join the skirt pieces (C) together, stitching on the straight grain. Press the seams open.

7 Join the frill pieces (D) together along the short edges. Turn under a double hem on the lower edge.

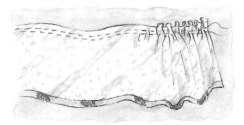

8 Run two rows of gathering stitches along the top edge of the frill. Working from both ends, pull the threads evenly so that the gathered fabric is the required size. Knot the threads. Pin the frill to the bottom of the skirt, right sides together. Tack in place, then stitch to secure.

9 Neaten the opening edges of the skirt with narrow double seams.

10 Fold the top edge of the skirt to the wrong side. Pin the heading tape close to the folded edge and stitch along both sides, tucking in the ends.

11 Knot one end of the gathering cords. From the opposite end, pull up the gathers until the fabric is the correct size. Add curtain hooks and hook onto the curtain track. Wind up the spare gathering cord. Place the scalloped top in position.

Bias strips were used to emphasize the stripes in the skirt fabric. If your dressing table does not have a curtain track, elasticize the skirt top and fix to the table with touch-and-close fastening.

SLIPPER CHAIR

The back of this cover is as
pretty as the front.

Measuring up

To the following measurements, add 1.5cm
(⅝in) for all seam allowances:
Outside back – Measure the depth and width
to the middle, plus 8cm (3in) for central
closure and closure hem allowances. Allow
two pieces (A).
Inside back – Measure width around padding,
and the depth, plus 2.5cm (1in) for a tuck-in
(B).
Seat – Measure depth plus 2.5cm (1in) for a
tuck-in, and width around padding (C); make
a paper pattern for the shape, see step 2.
Skirt – Measure the perimeter of the seat and
add half the total measurement for gathered
fullness plus 6cm (2½in) for closure hems;
measure the depth plus hem allowance (D).
Sash and tie (one for each piece) – Measure
the length from side edge of chair to middle
and add 68cm (27in) for the tie. Our width is
8cm (3in) (E).
Piping – Allow for bias strips (F).

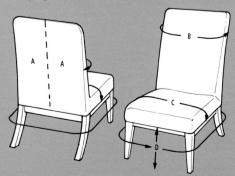

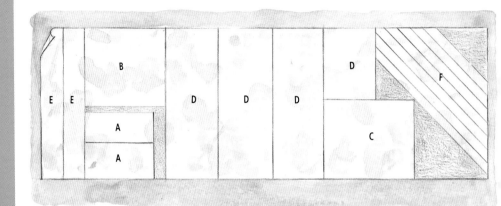

1 Using your measurements, mark
the cutting lines on the grain of the
fabric as shown and cut out. Mark
the letters on the pieces.

2 Place paper over the seat and
draw around, allowing for a tuck-in
at the inside back and extending the
sides to accommodate the depth of
the chair sides and back. Add seam
allowances. Place on the seat piece
(C) and cut out.

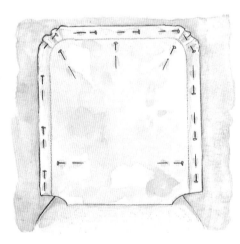

3 With wrong side out, position
the inside back (B) on the chair and
mark the seamline. Allow for the
tuck-in on the lower edge; curve the
fabric at each side of the tuck-in to
fit around the depth of the chair.

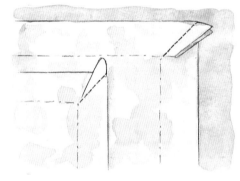

4 With the fabric still in place,
shape the shoulders by pinning the
excess fabric together. Remove and
stitch to form a dart, then trim
across.

5 Join the seat to the inside back,
stitching across the tuck-in and the
extensions at each side in one
continuous seam. Make darts on the
seat front as for the shoulders.

6 On the outside back sections
(A), neaten the back closure with
double hems, stitching along both
sides. Overlap the closure and tack
to hold. Treat as one piece. Pin to
the chair, curve the shoulders, mark
the seamline and trim.

7 Join the short sides of the skirt pieces (D) to make up the length but do not stitch to a circle. Stitch and press the seams open. Hem the lower edge. Neaten the side edges, which should align with the back closure.

8 Run two rows of gathering stitches along the top edge, stitching just within the seam allowance. Pull the gathers to fit and secure.

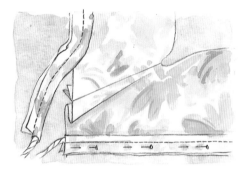

9 Make up sufficient piping for the inside back and the seat. Tack, then pin piping around the inside back, adding a small tuck at the back seat "gusset" to help with the fit. Cross over the piping ends, tack to secure.

10 Join the inside back to the outside back. Pin wrong sides together with the piping sandwiched between. Tack, then stitch close to the piping using the zipper foot.

11 Replace the cover wrong sides out. Pin on the skirt with the opening at the back. Tack and stitch.

12 Replace the cover right side out. Mark the button and buttonhole positions evenly down the back. Remove cover, sew buttonholes and attach the buttons.

13 For the sash and ties, fold each piece of fabric lengthways right sides together and stitch down the long sides. Sew one short end diagonally. Press seam open.

14 Turn right side out and press with the seam in the centre. Fold under the unsewn short end and pin both in place above the skirt line at the back, folded ends up against the piping. Stitch close to the edge.

The full gathered skirt adds to the soft lines of this chair.

FUTON COVER

This two-sided cover has an original toggle closure, with one side for seating and one side for sleeping.

CHECKLIST

Materials

two coordinating heavyweight
   furnishing fabrics: one patterned,
   one plain
long handsewing needle
fabric adhesive
general sewing equipment   page 110–11

Techniques

machine stitching   page 114–15

Measuring up

To the following measurements, add 1.5cm
(⅝in) seam allowances:
Futon top (patterned fabric) – Measure the
length and width, going halfway down the
sides of the mattress, plus an opening end
hem allowance (A).
Futon bottom (plain fabric) – The same
measure as A and 15cm (6in) for the pocket
flap, plus an opening end hem allowance (B).
Toggle fastenings – In patterned fabric, allow
3 bias strips about 4cm (1½in) wide by 66cm
(26in) long. In plain fabric, allow 3 bias strips
4cm (1½in) wide by 18cm (7in) long (C).

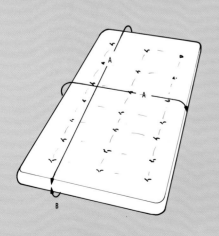

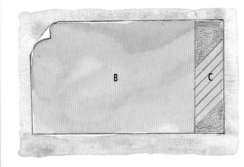

1 Using your measurements, mark the cutting lines on the grain of the fabric and cut out.

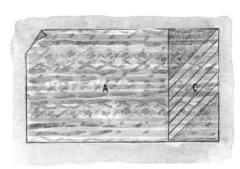

2 On the top section (A), neaten one short edge with a narrow hem. Repeat for the bottom section (B), this time snipping into the seam allowance at each side.

3 With right sides together, pin and stitch the top and bottom sections together around the sides.

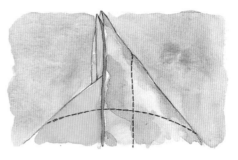

4 Fold the pocket flap to the wrong side, level with the top section. Handstitch in place, attaching the corners to the side seams with one or two firm stitches.

5 To accommodate the depth of the mattress, stitch across the bottom two corners of the cover. Working on the wrong side, place the two seams together and stitch in a curve to the measurements given.

6 For the toggle fastenings, press the raw edges of all the bias strips to the wrong side, then fold the strips in half lengthways, right side out. Press, then stitch. To prevent fraying, treat the ends with fabric adhesive.

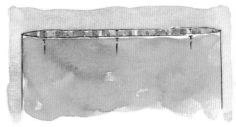

7 Mark the loop positions on the inside edge of the pocket flap fold. Mark the corresponding position of the toggles on the top section.

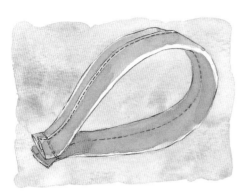

10 Handstitch the toggles in place, stitching through the looped end. Alternatively, the cover can be secured with snap fasteners.

8 Form the plain fabric loops and stitch across the ends to neaten. Handstitch in position to secure.

9 For the toggles, coil the strips around themselves four times, leaving the middle wide enough to insert the strip. Pass the end through the middle and bring it back, leaving a 5cm (2in) loop. Cut off. Using a long needle, sew in place through the middle to secure.

The large surface area of a futon is ideal for displaying your favourite fabric.

ACCESSORIES

Loose covers can be put on more than just sofas and chairs, and the projects in this chapter show the variety of treatments that can be achieved with just about any piece of furniture and any type of fabric. If you want something very simple, there are projects for winter and summer that involve almost no sewing, while the instructions for tassels will help to complete any loose cover with a professional look.

FOOTSTOOL COVER

Change the look of your footstool with a floor length cover made from a cream damask fabric, which will coordinate with any interior.

C H E C K L I S T

Materials

furnishing fabric
lining fabric
pre-shrunk piping cord
general sewing equipment   page 110–11

Techniques

piping and binding   page 118–19
inverted pleats   page 120–21

Measuring up

To the following measurements, add 1.5cm (⅝in) for all seam allowances:
Top panel – Measure the length and the depth (A).
Skirt (long sides) – Measure depth plus hem allowance and width plus 10cm (4in) pleat allowance (B) in fabric and lining.
Skirt (short sides) – Measure depth plus hem allowance and width plus 10cm (4in) pleat allowance (C) in fabric and lining.
Inverted pleats – Allow four pieces: depth is same measure as B, width is 10cm (4in) (D) in fabric and lining.
Piping – Allow for bias strips (E).

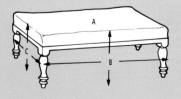

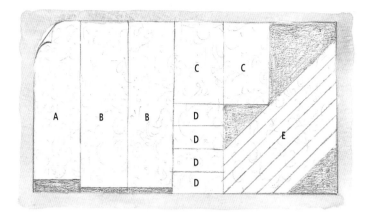

1 Using your measurements, mark the cutting lines for each section on the grain of the fabric and cut out. Mark the letters on each piece.

2 Make up sufficient piping to go around the top of the stool. With right sides together, tack it to the top panel. Snip into the piping seam allowance at each corner.

3 Using skirt and pleat pieces as templates, cut out the skirt lining. Tack the lining and skirt sections right sides together and stitch across the lower edge. Turn to the right side and press.

4 Join the skirt pieces (B and C) together placing a pleat piece (D) between them at the corners. Neaten the seams together.

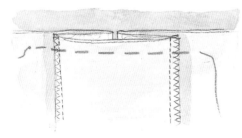

5 From the right side, make an inverted pleat at the corners so that the seams are on the inside fold of the pleat. Stitch across the top edge to hold, then press.

6 Pin the skirt to the top panel, right sides together, with the piping sandwiched between. Tack carefully, especially around the pleats. Using the zipper foot, stitch as close to the piping as possible. Remove the tacking stitches and press the seam away from the top panel.

STITCHING THROUGH SEVERAL LAYERS

While most modern sewing machines will cope well with stitching through several layers of fabric, it is important to tack all bulky seams carefully to prevent them from slipping and spoiling the effect.

When machine stitching, shorten the stitch length at the corners and stitch slowly, using the handwheel for better control.

Bulky seam allowances can be layered. To do this, shorten each layer progressively so that the deepest seam allowance will fall next to the main fabric when the seam is pressed and turned to the right side.

This piece of furniture can be used as both a footrest and a coffee table so a cover that can be removed for cleaning is ideal.

BLANKET BOX COVER

This clever cover stays on while you lift the lid so you can have extra storage and seating with style.

C H E C K L I S T

Materials

closely woven furnishing fabric
contrast fabric for bows
pre-shrunk piping cord
touch-and-close fastening
general sewing equipment   page 110–11

Techniques

piping and binding   page 118–19

Measuring up

To the following measurements, add 1.5cm (⅝in) seam allowances:
Front – Measure the width and depth, plus hem allowance top and bottom (A).
Sides – Measure the width and depth, plus hem allowance top and bottom (B).
Back and outside lid – Measure the width and depth from the floor at the back (plus hem) to the edge of the lid at the front (C).
Inside lid – Measure the width and depth (D).
Lid gusset – Measure width and depth (E).
Piping – Allow for bias strips (F).
Bows – Allow for bias strips (G).

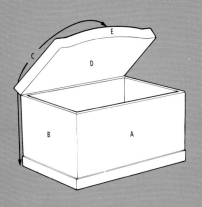

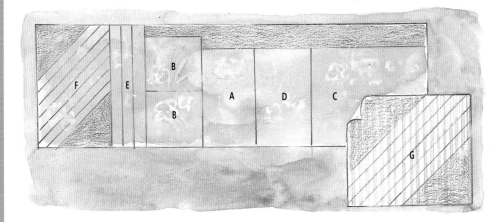

1 Using your measurements, mark the cutting lines on the grain of the fabric and cut out. Mark the letters on each piece.

2 Place the back and outside lid section (C) on the box, wrong side out, and mark the depth between the hinges and the top edge of the cushion with tacking stitches.

3 Stitch the gusset pieces (E) together along the short edges to make up the required length. Neaten the short ends. Make up enough piping for the lid gusset, top and bottom edges.

4 Tack the top lid piping in place. At the front corners, snip into the piping seam allowance.

5 With right sides together and corners matching, tack the gusset to the outside lid piece on three sides. Stitch close to the piping.

6 Neaten the back edge of the inside lid (D) with a narrow hem. Apply piping as in step 4, then stitch to the gusset.

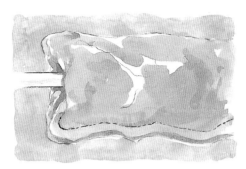

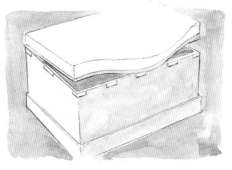

7 On the outside lid, neaten the short sides at the back edges (cushion depth) with a narrow hem.

8 With right sides together, stitch the two side pieces (B) to the front piece (A). Press the seams open. Neaten the top edge with a narrow hem.

10 For the bows, join the short ends of the strips as required for length. With right sides together, press in half lengthways, then stitch the long sides and one short end. Turn right side out with the help of a knitting needle, then stitch the remaining short ends closed. Press, then tie into bows. Handstitch at the corners of the cover.

11 To keep the cover in place, stitch small strips of touch-and-close fastening around the top edge of the cover and attach at the corresponding points on the box.

9 Stitch the front and side sections to the back-outside lid section, aligning the top edge of the front with the marked hinge line on the back. Press the seams open. Hem the lower edges, then press.

The inside lid piece can be made with curtain lining or sheeting to cut down on costs.

SQUARE TABLECOVER

Dress up your folding tables for the festive season, or any other special occasion.

C H E C K L I S T

Materials

heavyweight silk or taffeta
  furnishing fabric
general sewing equipment   page 110–11

Techniques

slip hemstitching   page 112–13
inverted pleats   page 120–21

Measuring up

To the following measurements, add 1.5cm (⅝in) seam allowances:
Top – Measure in all directions (A).
Skirt – Measure the width of each side and add pleat allowances; ours measure 16cm (6¼in) each. Measure the depth and add the hem allowance (B).

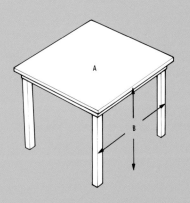

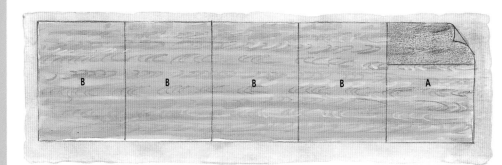

1 Using your measurements, mark the cutting lines on the grain of the fabric and cut out. Mark the letters on each piece.

2 With right sides together, pin, tack and stitch the skirt pieces along the side seams. Trim the seam allowance to 1cm (⅜in) and neaten the edges. Press the seams to one side.

3 To mark where the folds of the pleats will fall, measure 4cm (1½in) to the right of each side seam and mark with an 'X', and 12cm (4¾in) to the left and mark with a 'Y'.

4 Fold the fabric at Y and X and bring them together on the right side of the fabric. The side seams should fall on a hidden fold. Tack to secure.

5 Snip into the centre of the seam allowance for each pleat to allow for easing around the corners. With wrong sides together, pin the skirt to the top section so that the raw edges match and the centre of each pleat aligns with its corresponding corner.

6 Tack, then stitch, pivoting the needle at each corner before stitching the next side. Trim, neaten the seams together and press.

7 Place the cover inside out on the table and mark the hemline. Remove and turn under a double hem, pressing and pinning. Slip hemstitch by hand.

To simplify the sewing, this cover was made without piping but you could add piping along the tabletop seam; a contrast colour would look good here (see Piping and Binding, pages 118–19).

WEDDINGCAKE TABLECOVER

A special cover for a special event, and almost as pretty as a bridal gown.

C H E C K L I S T

Materials

cotton chintz and plain cotton fabric
satin ribbon and picot edged ribbon
lace
pearl strip
fabric adhesive (optional)
iron-on fusible webbing
paper for pattern

Techniques

machine stitching   page 114–15

Measuring up

Full cover – Measure the diameter of the table (A) plus the depth from the edge of the table to the floor (B). To calculate the total fabric amount, double the measurement B and add a hem allowance.
Top cover – Measurement A, plus desired overhang allowance.

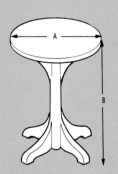

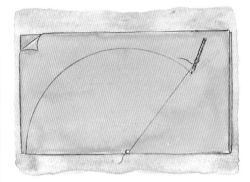

1 Fold the full cover fabric in half. Working on a firm surface, draw a semi-circle using a compass made from a length of string (cut to the radius length) attached to a pencil. Cut through all layers.

2 Turn under a hem all around the bottom. Stitch or use fabric adhesive to secure.

3 Place the cover on the table and position the lace around the bottom edge, pinning to secure. Cover the top edge of the lace with a row of pearl strip, topped with satin ribbon. Stitch all the trimmings, or tack and secure with fabric adhesive.

4 For the top cover, shape the fabric into a circle using your measurements, see step 1. Zigzag the raw edge and cover with the picot edge ribbon, stitching it to secure.

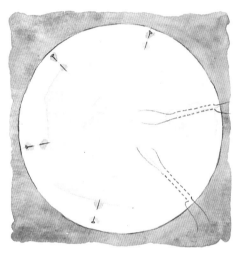

5 To gather the top cloth, divide the circumference into six – fold three times and mark the edges of the folds with pins. Run machine gathering stitches in lines radiating towards the middle, stopping level with the table edge.

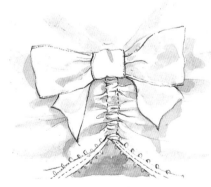

6 Pull up the gathering threads evenly and fasten off the ends. Make six bows, and attach with one or two stitches at the top of the gathers.

INSPIRATIONS
Taking the simple bottom cover
and top cloth as your base, there
is no limit to the embellishing
you can do. Fabrics such as lace,
netting, satin and silk can all be
used, and more elaborate
touches, such as dried or silk
flowers and beaded bridal
appliqués, can be added to match
the bride's dress. Browse through
the bridal fabrics and trimmings
section of a department store to
pick up ideas.

*This cover is simple
to make and the
effect is stunning;
just the thing to
personalize a
wedding reception.*

SCROLL-SHAPED ARM CAPS

Use coordinating fabric to protect the arms of your sofa or chair and prolong the life of your cover or upholstery.

C H E C K L I S T

Materials

closely woven furnishing fabric
pre-shrunk piping cord
paper for pattern
general sewing equipment   page 110–11

Techniques

piping and binding   page 118–19

Measuring up

To the following measurements, add 1.5cm (⅝in) seam allowances:
Main section – Measure length and width (A).
Front arm – Measure the length and depth (B); make a paper pattern for the shape, see step 2.
Piping – Allow for bias strips (C).
NOTE: Remember to allow for a pair.

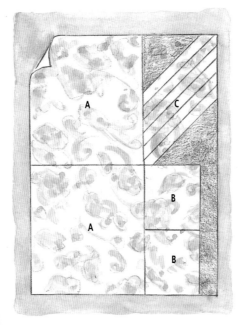

1 Using your measurements, mark the cutting lines on the grain of the fabric and match any pattern on the arm cap fabric to that on the existing cover. Cut out and mark the letters on each piece.

2 Lay paper over the front arm and trace around the shape. Cut out one fabric piece, then cut the other using the paper pattern in reverse. Zigzag the straight edges.

3 Make up sufficient piping to go along the front edges of the two main pieces. Zigzag all but the front edges of main section.

4 With right sides together and raw edges matching, pin, tack and stitch the piping in place on the two main section pieces.

5 Working with the fabric wrong side out and the piping at the front, put one main section on the arm of the chair. Position one front arm and pin. Remove and tack. Repeat for the other arm.

6 Before stitching, make a single narrow turning on the lower edges of the front arms at one side only, where they meet the long edge of the main section.

7 Using the zipper foot, stitch the seam joining the main piece to the front arms. Remove tacking, zigzag to neaten and press the seam away from the front arms.

Coordinating fabric was used for these arm caps but if matching fabric is not available, they look just as good in contrast fabric.

8 Make a single narrow turning around the remaining edges and mitre the corners.

9 Tack, then stitch starting at the inner back corner and working around the front edge. Stitch along the piping, pivoting the fabric at the inner corner. Press.

SUMMER INSPIRATIONS

Warm lazy days go hand in hand with easy to create interior styles. Here we offer a glimpse of just a few of the covers that can be made with lightweight fabrics and cool printed sheets. No need for fussy shaping and seaming to achieve these looks and they are just the thing to help pass the warm summer months with style.

▶ *The lacy layered look on this table is easily achieved. A plain ready-made round tablecloth is topped with an oversized square lace cloth and the excess lace is swept up at the corners and secured with bows. We chose complementary neutral tones to keep the summery feel but a dark cloth beneath the lace would be equally as stunning.*

◀ *This small padded stool was covered with a round tablecloth and tied with a wide sash made from coordinating fabric. To get the attractive effect of fabric puddling on the floor, use an oversized cloth.*

◄ A large flat sheet in cheerful, summery print was draped over this wicker chair. The excess fabric was brought around to the back and all the ends were tied and tucked in attractively. A cushion is used to secure the sheet and keep the wrapping intact.

► This wrought iron garden chair is dressed for a special occasion with a large length of extra wide sheer fabric, knotted at the seat with a large satin ribbon. A lacy cushion is both a festive and functional addition, making this chair just the thing for an outdoor wedding celebration. Curtain fabric was used for this treatment, but any sheer fabric, such as chiffon, could also be used.

WINTER INSPIRATIONS

As the days get shorter and the weather cooler, a warm cosy interior becomes more appealing. Heat up your home with some of the simple styles shown here, using heavy fabrics or deep colours and, with very little sewing, create a snug comfortable atmosphere for relaxing on cold winter nights.

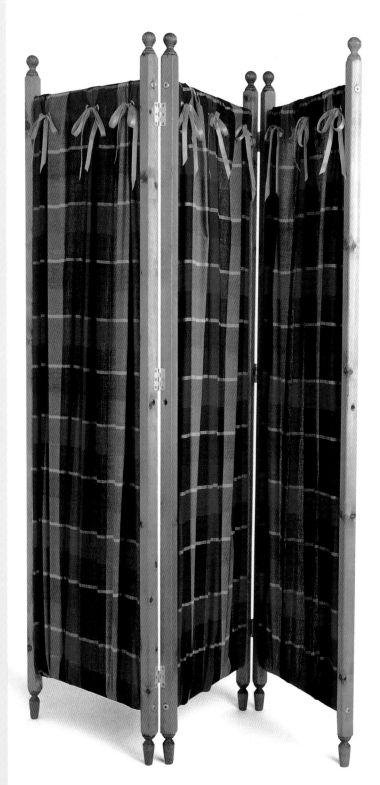

◀ *Keep out the cold with a warming screen that is a cinch to create on any type of frame. Determine the fabric position and match any stripes, then cut the lengths. The top end is secured by passing coordinating ribbon through eyelet holes and the bottom end can be sewn, stapled or nailed depending on the design of your screen.*

◄ *Dress up your chairs for the holiday season. Here, an upholstered upright chair was covered in a sheet that has been stencilled with gold stars using fabric paint. Secure the sheet by tying it to the back of the chair with a long length of cord and add tassels to the ends to complete the festive look.*

▼ *When the cold weather sets in, warm up your interior by cloaking your furniture in cosy tones of velvet. Here, a long length of rich blue velvet was draped over a footstool and then caught up at the corners for a gentle swag effect. Secure the fabric at each corner with a few invisible tacking stitches.*

STITCHED HEAD TASSEL

Tassels are an attractive addition to a piece of soft furnishing, whether a sofa throw, cushion or curtain arrangement.

CHECKLIST

Materials

yarn or embroidery thread (one or
  two colours)
stiff card
wadding
tapestry needle
general sewing equipment   page 110–11

1 Cut a piece of card to the chosen length of the tassel and approximately 5–7.5cm (2–3in) wide. Wind the yarn around the card between twenty and forty times – the higher the figure the more solid and thick the tassel.

2 Cut the threads along one edge of the card. Keep the strands folded in half and thread a needle with doubled yarn. Pass the looped end around the strands, take the needle through the loop and pull firmly. Bring the needle out below.

3 Tease out small pieces of wadding and push them inside the head of the tassel. Keep adding wadding until the head is a well-rounded shape.

4 Thread the needle as in step 2 and bind the tassel head in the same way. Pull tightly and take the needle up through the head and out at the top of the tassel. Leave these threads uncut for attaching the tassel.

5 For the overstitching, thread the needle with the desired colour (either the same or contrast). Knot the other end and pull up the centre of the tassel head, coming out at the top of the tassel head. Work buttonhole stitches all around the head, working in continuous rows and placing the stitches in the loops of the previous row. Trim the ends.

BALL TASSEL

The ball makes it easier to form a neat, round shape for your tassels.

CHECKLIST

Materials

paper or polystyrene ball
stranded embroidery thread or
   cotton perle
tapestry needle
general sewing equipment   page 110–11

1 Enlarge the central hole of the paper ball by digging out the centre until the hole is about half the size of the ball itself.

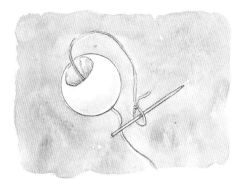

2 Thread the tapestry needle with one end of a skein of embroidery thread. Make a small loop in the opposite end. Take the needle through the ball and thread through the loop; pull tight to fasten the thread around the ball.

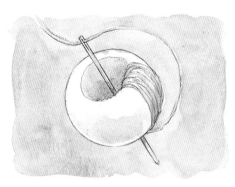

3 Wind the thread around the ball, forming a smooth covering, until it is totaly covered. Add a second layer as desired. Fasten off the thread underneath the ball.

4 Make the tail as for the stitched head tassel, step 2.

5 Take the ends of the binding threads through the hole in the ball form the hanging loop, and pull up to take the tail end inside the ball. Fasten off the ends.

6 Comb out the tassel and trim the strands level.

SIMPLE TASSEL

An easy-to-make tassel for informal decors.

CHECKLIST

Materials

yarn
stiff card
tapestry needle
general sewing equipment   page 110–11

1 Wind the yarn around the card as for the stitched head tassel (see step 1).

2 Cut a length of the same yarn and thread onto the needle. Slide this under the threads at the top end of the card. Wrap around the threads several times, then tie the ends together, gathering up the threads firmly. Leave the needle and yarn hanging. Cut through the loops at the opposite end.

3 To make a matching twisted cord for hanging, cut several lengths of yarn to three times the desired finished length. Knot the strands together at each end. Secure one end around a doorknob and slide a pencil in the other end. Twist the pencil until the strands are tight.

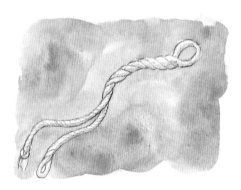

4 Remove from the doorknob and fold the strands in half; they will twist together tightly forming the cord. Shake vigorously to get the twists even. Knot the ends together.

5 With the length of thread already attached, bind the strands around to form the head of the tassel, approximately one quarter down from the top. Fasten off the binding thread.

6 Open out the strands and thread the loop end of the cord under the binding threads. Fold the strands back again to cover the knot.

7 Trim the ends to an even length.

Use tassels with decorative cord to embellish your soft furnishings.

TECHNIQUES

This chapter deals simply and thoroughly with every technique you will need to make the projects in this book. When specialized knowledge is required, you will find explanations of loose cover making methods in the section called Working With Fabric. There is also information about the necessary equipment, all of which is widely available.

BASIC EQUIPMENT

IN THE same way that you would prepare your workspace before beginning a major home-furnishing project, having the right basic equipment will also contribute to the efficiency and success of your project. When you buy tools and supplies, always choose the best quality available to ensure high performance and durability.

Table: For handling the large amounts of fabric necessary for making loose covers, a large work table is a pre-requisite. For cutting out fabric, a clean floor space is a good alternative.

Large, fold-away dressmaker's cutting-out boards are available. They are marked with a grid to help keep right angles when cutting. This can be placed temporarily on a smaller table when a larger permanent work table is not practical.

Cutting-out shears: These should be heavy-duty shears with long, strong blades (about 20cm/8in is an ideal length) and with bent handles that allow the blades to lie flat on the cutting surface.

Pinking shears: The edges of these blades are serrated and cut with a zigzag edge. They are excellent for finishing (neatening) the edges of certain seam allowances.

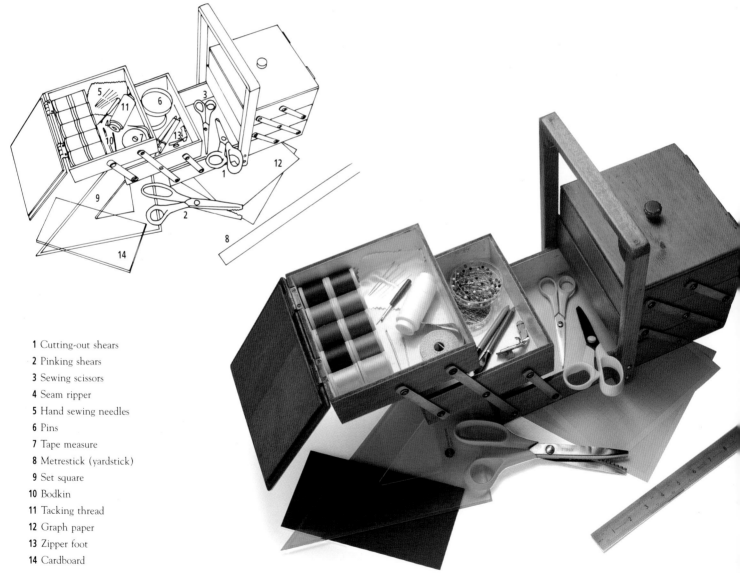

1 Cutting-out shears

2 Pinking shears

3 Sewing scissors

4 Seam ripper

5 Hand sewing needles

6 Pins

7 Tape measure

8 Metrestick (yardstick)

9 Set square

10 Bodkin

11 Tacking thread

12 Graph paper

13 Zipper foot

14 Cardboard

Sewing scissors: These scissors have small sturdy blades and are useful for clipping into seams, trimming fabric and threads.

Seam ripper: This has a sharp, curved edge for cutting seams open and a point for picking out loose threads. It is handy for removing tacking threads.

Hand sewing needles: These needles are the all-purpose needles used in hand sewing. They have long, sharp points, round eyes and come in a variety of sizes.

Pins: In addition to the standard size dressmaker's stainless steel pins, long, 3cm (1¼in) pins or T-shaped pins are handy for sewing home furnishing projects. These longer pins with large heads make it easier to pin fabrics together or fit it to upholstered furniture.

Tape measure: This tool is essential for taking measurements around a piece of furniture. The best choice is the flexible variety that will not stretch.

Carpenter's metrestick (yardstick): This is ideal for long straight measurements such as marking off bias strips, checking straight grainlines and for measuring the skirt height from floor to seamline.

Set square: A set square is useful for measuring 45° and 90° angles and is extremely helpful in marking fabric on the bias (across the grain).

Bodkin: This is a flat needle with a very large eye used for threading elastic, cord or tape through a casing.

Tailor's chalk: Available in block or pencil form in a range of colours, tailor's chalk is used for all fabric marking and is easily brushed off after use.

Tacking thread: Available in white only, this soft, loosely twisted cotton is used for hand tacking. It breaks easily and can be removed quickly from a project.

Heavy-duty thread: For sewing upholstery fabrics by hand or machine, choose cotton, polyester or cotton-wrapped polyester threads for extra strength and durability.

Iron: A combination steam/dry iron is very useful for all home sewing projects. Where possible, press on the wrong side to avoid putting a shine on fabric. If you need to press on the right side, use a pressing cloth to prevent this.

Dressmaker's graph paper: This is available in packs of several one size sheets: about 90cm × 60cm (36in × 24in). It is marked with an all-over grid in metric measurements to facilitate making paper patterns to a specific size and shape.

Sewing machine: A sewing machine is an invaluable piece of equipment for sewing home furnishings and here, the modern machine should be used to full advantage. In the past, where some techniques were done by hand, they are now better done by machine; for example, hemming.

Zipper foot: This sewing machine attachment is invaluable for inserting zips and for stitching piping into seams.

Cardboard: A rectangle of 6mm (¼in) thick cardboard – about 20cm × 10cm (8in × 4in) – is used to push down the tuck-ins into the narrow crevices around the seat and inside back arms on sofas and armchairs.

Alternatively, if you do not have cardboard, a clean wooden spatula will do the job just as effectively.

HAND STITCHING

THE FINISH of a loose cover depends largely on using the best technique for the task. Careful cutting out and seaming are essential and, in order to hold the seams and large expanses of fabric secure until they are permanently stitched, hand sewing is necessary.

Other hand-sewn operations include shaping – perhaps on the shoulders of an armchair cover – where fabric fullness is reduced by gathering using running stitches; joining patterned and striped fabric together using ladder stitch, and for securing deep hems where the stitching should not show on the right side.

When working with furnishing fabrics, you will need a selection of sharp, multi-purpose sewing needles, matching heavy-duty sewing threads to suit the type of fabric being used, and a thimble for the middle finger of the sewing hand. For heavier fabrics, use heavy-duty tacking cotton.

Tacking
Tacking is used to temporarily hold together fabric layers during the construction of a project, or to mark a fold line, hemline or skirt level more permanently than chalk.

Catch stitch
This stitch is useful for holding facings in place, or for making a hem in thick fabric where a second turning would be bulky. Wadding is sometimes held to a seam allowance with this stitch if it is not possible to sew through the wadding.

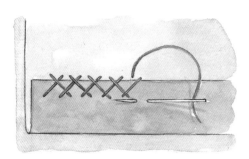

1 Working from left to right, make a small horizontal stitch in the upper layer of fabric, followed by a small horizontal stitch in the lower layer diagonally across the first stitch. Continue in this way, keeping the thread loose.

Ladder stitch
A temporary stitch worked on the right side of the fabric, which allows precise matching of stripes and large patterned fabrics at seamlines.

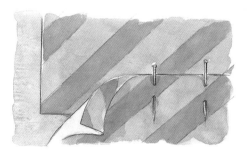

1 Press under the seam allowance on one piece of fabric. Position this piece over the other so that the raw edges are even and the pattern matches exactly. Pin them together.

2 Working from the right side with the thread secured within the folded edge (with a knot), take the needle directly across to the flat piece of fabric and take it underneath, along the seamline, for about 1.5cm ($\frac{5}{8}$in).

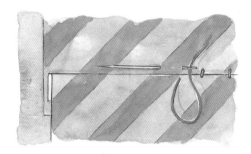

3 Pull the thread through and take the needle directly across to the folded edge. Slip it underneath, as before, and repeat.

Running stitch

This simplest of stitches is used mainly for gathering small amounts of fullness – on the shoulder of a sofa cover, for example.

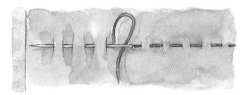

⚠ Working from right to left, weave the needle in and out of the fabric several times before pulling the thread through. Make both the stitches, and the spaces between, small and even.

Hemming stitch

This stitch is used for securing all types of hems and for finishing the underside of a bound edge.

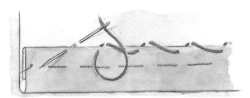

⚠ Fold the hem or binding to the wrong side. Pin and tack it to the required depth. Working from right to left, take a tiny stitch in the fabric and, without pulling the thread through, take another small stitch through the fold of the hem. Pull the thread through. Insert the needle directly below the first stitch and repeat, spacing the stitches about 5mm ($\frac{3}{16}$in) apart.

Blind stitch

Used for sewing hems and facings in place. The stitches are hidden between the layers of fabric and are invisible from the right side, which gives a true professional finish.

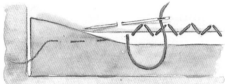

⚠ Tack the layers to be stitched. As you work, fold back 3mm ($\frac{1}{8}$in) of the top edge and, holding the needle horizontally, take a tiny stitch, first through the bottom layer, then the top layer. Repeat, keeping a fairly loose tension.

Slip hemming

A neat and durable stitch used on hems and other folded edges such as binding.

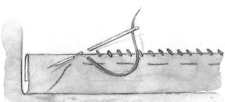

⚠ Prepare the hem or folded edge and tack in place. Make a tiny stitch in the main fabric, under a single thread, close to the hem. Without pulling the thread through, slip the needle into the folded edge close to the first stitch, bring it out just to the left, and repeat.

Slip stitch

This stitch is used to join two folded edges together, such as on a cushion cover or to complete a seam that has been left partly open for turning through.

⚠ Tack the two folded edges together. Holding the fabric folds upwards, and working from right to left, bring the needle into the nearer fold and make a stitch about 3mm ($\frac{1}{8}$in) long. Without pulling the thread through, take a similar stitch in the opposite fold, pull the thread through and repeat. The stitches should be almost invisible.

Machine stitching

A SEWING MACHINE is the most essential piece of equipment for sewing home furnishings, and for loose covers in particular. Where there is considerable strain put on a seam, as on loose covers for sofas and armchairs, a machine-stitched seam is both stronger and easier to handle (since the weight of the fabric is supported by the work table); it is also much quicker than sewing by hand.

Your machine does not have to be elaborate, but it should be sturdy enough to cope with medium and/or heavyweight fabrics and heavy-duty sewing threads and needles. Most sewing machines come with various attachments for special tasks, such as a zipper foot for stitching in zips and piping cord, and a gathering foot – which is helpful for gathering long lengths of fabric. For most soft furnishings, a plain seam is all that is required and, if your machine has the facility for zigzag stitch, you can neaten seams in the appropriate way for most furnishing fabrics.

Before starting a project, it is advisable to stitch-test a piece of fabric and, if necessary, adjust the tension, stitch length, thread and needle. If you have doubts, refer to your sewing machine manual.

Straight stitch

Most machines will produce straight stitches that vary in length. The smallest stitches are used on fine fabrics and the longest for gathering and machine tacking. Where there is a swing needle, the length and width can be varied to suit different tasks and different fabrics.

Zigzag stitch

A medium zigzag stitch is used for neatening the seams of fabrics that fray easily, and a wider, closer one for neatening seams together.

Machine tacking

If your machine has this facility, then it would be advantageous to use it, especially on long straight seams prior to machine stitching.

Plain seam

This is the most commonly used seam. It is worked by stitching two or more layers of fabric together then pressing the seam allowances either open or to one side, and neatening them in an appropriate way. It can be straight, curved or cornered. The seam allowance for home furnishings is usually 1.5cm ($\frac{5}{8}$in).

1 For a plain seam, pin the two pieces of fabric together, right sides facing and raw edges even. Tack just inside the seamline using even tacking stitches.

2 Using a stitch length suitable for the fabric, stitch following the seamline. Remove the tacking, press the seam flat to sink the stitches, then press it open.

Curved seams

The edges of a curved seam are clipped or notched so that they will lie flat when pressed. If the seam is to be pressed flat, clip the seam allowance; if the curved seam is to be enclosed, notch the allowance so that they will not overlap when turned to the right side.

Corners

To stitch around a corner, you should pivot the fabric around the needle.

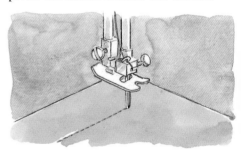

1 At the corner, stop the machine and leave the needle down in the fabric. Raise the presser foot and turn the fabric, aligning the new seamline. Lower the presser foot and continue stitching.

2 Where there is a seam at the corner, strengthen the seam by shortening the stitches for a short distance at each side.

Joining corners

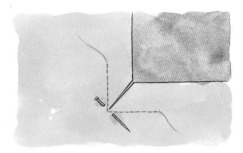

1 To join an inward corner to an outward corner, first reinforce the inward corner, stitching just inside the seamline at either side of the corner. Pin across the point where the stitches form the angle. Clip up to, but not past, the stitches.

2 Spread the clipped section so that it fits the other edge and pin in position. With the clipped side up, stitch on the seamline pivoting the fabric at the corner.

Neatening seam allowances

Used on fabrics that fray where the seam is exposed.

1 First make a line of straight stitching about 1cm (⅜in) from the seam on each allowance. Then trim the edge with pinking shears close to the stitching.

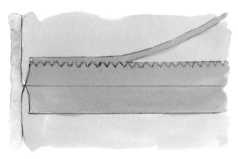

2 Alternatively, zigzag stitch near to the edge of the seam allowance, then trim close to the stitching.

Overstitching

The instructions in certain projects may call for neatening two seam allowances together. To do this, press the seam flat and trim as instructed, then stitch close to the edge using a wide zigzag stitch to lock the two raw edges together.

Machine-stitched hem

A machine-stitched hem is often used when neither a deep nor an inconspicuous hem is required. For example, on the unlined gathered frill of a kitchen chair cover.

1 Mark the hemline, turn under the fabric as instructed in the project and press. Turn under the edge again and press along the hemline. Tack in place.

2 Machine stitch close to the folded edge, keeping a straight line.

Stitching through several layers

Where several seam allowances intersect, or lining and main fabric seams are bulky, it is essential to layer some of them to reduce the bulk and make stitching easier.

1 Tack carefully to hold the fabric securely and stitch, first loosening the tension slightly and reducing the stitching speed. Where the fabrics are thickest, stitch manually (slower), using the handwheel.

2 Cut the seam allowances to different widths, with the seam allowance that will fall nearest the main fabric side cut the widest.

Machine-made buttonholes

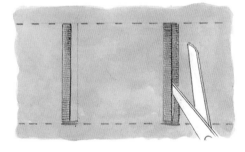

Although different machines may have different buttonhole mechanisms, essentially, the position of the buttonhole is first marked with tacking stitches, then vertical rows of zigzag stitch are worked on both sides. Before you work the second side, work a bar tack across the end and finish with another on the opposite end. Cut through the middle, to finish the buttonhole.

SECURING AND FASTENING

A LOOSE COVER requires an opening, essentially to facilitate its being removed easily for cleaning purposes.

On an armchair cover, the opening is usually positioned in one of the side back seams and, on a sofa cover, in either one or both side back seams. Generally speaking, an opening should cover at least three-quarters of the seam and align with the skirt opening but, in the case where a zip is used to close the main cover, the zip should not extend into the skirt.

On box cushion covers, the zip should be inserted at the back of the boxing strip, and should be long enough to go across the back and around at least one corner, to make it easier to get on and off.

An opening may be finished in one of the following ways using a zip, touch-and-close or press stud tape, or hooks and eyes. It is best to decide on the type of closure at the beginning of a project so that necessary fabric allowances can be made for facings and underlaps.

Applying a zip

1 A zip requires a centred application, and the opening seam allowances should be at least 3cm (1¼in) wide.

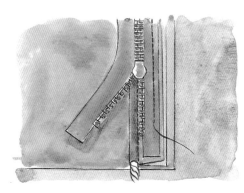

2 First open the zip, then place it face down on the right side of the opening, over the piping seam allowance if any, with the top stop 3cm (1¼in) above the lower seamline. Position the teeth close to the stitching, then tack and stitch.

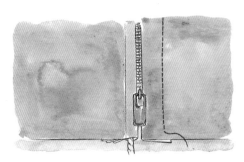

3 Turn under one edge and close the zip. Turn under the other opening edge and place it close to the stitching. Tack and stitch about 1cm (⅜in) away from the folded edge of the turning. Remove the tacking.

Applying touch-and-close tape

1 As the two halves of the tape need to overlap in order to lock the nylon hooks and loops securely, a lapped closure is required and a double-width seam allowance should be cut for the underlap on the opening edge. The standard seam allowance should be wider than the tape, for extra strength. The tape is best applied separately to each side of the opening seam.

2 Fold under the opening edge (outside arm side) to make the overlap and position the looped tape, right side up, over the piping. Tack and stitch around each side and, on the outer edge, close to the piping.

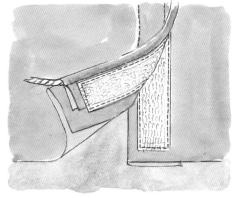

3 Fold under the other opening edge to make the underlap and position the hooked tape close to the edge, as shown. Tack and stitch around. Stitch across the top of the opening seam to finish.

Applying press stud tape

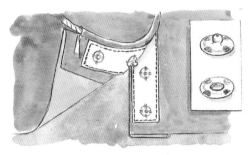

Fold under the opening edges to form the underlap and the overlap, and apply the tape in the same way as for touch-and-close tape. Place the socket tape on the underlap and the ball tape on the overlap.

ZIPS FOR BOX CUSHIONS

The zip is inserted at the back of the cushion cover into the gusset and taken around both back corners. For the length of the back gusset, allow fabric for the finished width of the cushion, plus the desired corner return (about 8cm/3in is usual), plus seam allowances, and the finished depth, plus seam allowances for the cushion and zip.

Hooks and eyes

1 This type of closure requires an overlap application. Allow two straight-cut pieces of fabric the length of the opening plus seam allowances, by 7.5cm (3in) wide. This is the ideal fastener for covers with gathered skirts.

2 Bind the opening with the strips of fabric: stitch right sides together, fold the strips in half to the wrong side, and press. Stitch through from the right side, close to the edge.

3 Fold the binding on the outside arm to the inside of the cover, and sew the hooks to the cover, level with the fold. Leave the binding on the outside back so that it extends and becomes the underlap. Sew on the eyes level with the inner edge of the binding.

Securing the bottom edge of a loose cover

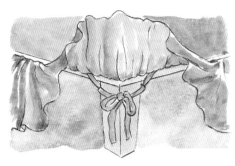

A very simple way of holding a skirted loose cover in place is to insert 30cm (12in) lengths of strong (twill) tape at each side of the leg positions during sewing. Alternatively, pieces of tape can be hand stitched to the seam using strong sewing thread and several overcasting stitches made in the same place. Cross the tape behind the leg, bring it to the front and tie in a double knot to secure.

PIPING AND BINDING

CORDED PIPING, which gives an attractive professional-looking finish to seamlines, is used on many home furnishings. On loose covers, it is advisable to pipe all the main exposed seams. Piping makes a seam stronger than a plain seam and also helps to define the edges of the cover, whether matching or contrast fabric is used. As a rule, piping should be applied first to the half of the seam that requires most control, before it is stitched to another. For example, you would add piping to a box cushion top before sewing on the side gussets.

Binding can also be used without piping cord to hem and give a neat finish. It is particularly attractive to choose a contrasting colour as a design feature.

Ready-made bias-binding can be bought in a range of colours and widths, and has the edges folded ready for sewing.

Preparing the bias strips

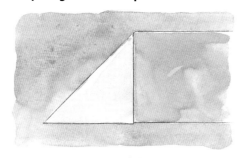

1 Press the fabric, then cut bias strips at a 45° angle to the selvedge. To find this angle, fold the cut edge of the fabric so that it is even with the selvedge and press along the fold.

2 Open and, using tailor's chalk and a ruler, mark along the crease. The width of the strips should be twice the seam allowance, plus three times the diameter of the piping cord. Measure this distance and mark all lines parallel to the first.

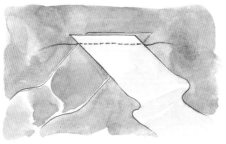

3 To make up the required length, join the individual strips on the straight grain. Place the two strips right sides together, pin and machine stitch across taking a 1.5cm (⅝in) seam. Trim the seam to 1cm (⅜in) and press the seam open.

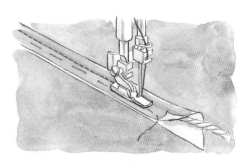

4 Fold the fabric strip in half and wrap it around the piping cord with the right side outside and with the raw edges matching. Using the zipper foot on your machine, stitch close to the cord.

MEASURING UP
To calculate how much piping cord and/or binding fabric are needed, first measure the edges you intend to pipe, add these for the total length and allow 3cm (1¼in) for joining the strips together, and at least another 2cm (¾in) for each end that will be stitched into a seam. For the amount of bias fabric needed, a quick calculation is to allow 1.4m (1½yd) for piping an armchair and 2.5m (2¾yd) for a sofa. Alternatively, allow approximately one-third less fabric than the length of your required fabric strip. For example, for a 120cm (48in) length of piping, you will need 90cm (36in) of fabric. It is important that the cord is pre-shrunk – if you are unsure, soak it in boiling water for several minutes and dry flat. A note: some cords may shrink as much as 25 per cent.

Piping a seam

1 Position the piping on the right side of your fabric to be seamed, with the stitching on the seamline and with the raw edges even. Tack in place about 3mm ($\frac{1}{8}$in) from the stitching. Using the zipper foot, stitch the piping in place working close to the previous stitching as shown. Press the stitched fabric flat.

2 On curved or angled edges, snip into the piping seam allowance to allow the finished seam to lie flat.

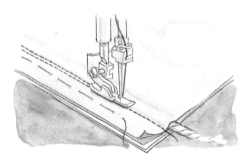

3 Position the corresponding section of fabric on top of the piped seam, right sides together, and tack. Turn the fabric over and, with the zipper foot, stitch between the cord and the first seamline. Notch the main seam allowance where the piping has been snipped, then turn right side out.

To join piping

1 Begin stitching the piping about 1.5cm ($\frac{5}{8}$in) in from the end and finish about 5cm (2in) from the starting point. Trim the overlapping cord so that the two ends meet exactly, and trim the fabric so that it overlaps the join by 1.5cm ($\frac{5}{8}$in).

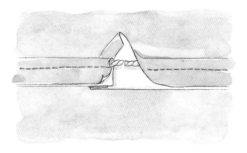

2 Fold under the trimmed fabric by 6mm ($\frac{1}{4}$in) and wrap this end around the starting end.

3 Stitch across both ends for a short distance beyond the starting point and, if necessary, backstitch to reinforce.

Neatening piping at an opening

1 To make the piping less bulky on an opening edge, remove about 2.5cm (1in) of cord nearest to the opening. Bring the seam allowances together over the cord, turn under the short end and continue the stitching.

2 Tack and stitch the hem on the opening edge, stitching smoothly over the piping now the cord has been removed.

Making binding

1 Lightly press the binding in half lengthways, wrong sides together, then press under the edges so that they almost touch the central crease line. If the binding is to be used on a curved edge, press it again, shaping it into a slight curve.

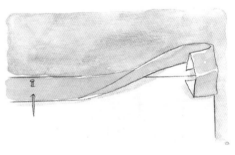

2 Before binding an edge, trim away the seam allowance (if one has been included) as it is not needed for this finish, then encase the raw edge and tack. Turn under the short raw edges, folding them towards the wrong side so that the edge of the main fabric is covered and neatened. Working from the right side, stitch along the edge of the binding through all layers.

FRILLS AND PLEATS

THE FINISHED style of your loose cover will depend largely on the type of skirt you choose. Simply by gathering or folding fabric in a variety of ways, a range of decorative skirt finishes can be created. A gathered frill on the edge of a floor-length tablecover or skirt on an armchair cover gives a soft, graceful line, while crisp pleats are used for more formal effects.

If you use either a directional fabric pattern, or a gathered or pleated skirt, the fabric will need to be joined from several sections to make up the necessary width and to ensure the fabric grain runs in the correct vertical direction. The sections are stitched together to make a continuous length or circle (depending on whether there is a closure), and then shortened to the required size by gathering or pleating.

A traditional tailored skirt with inverted pleats at the corners, however, is constructed in four sections – one at each side – where the seams can be made at the corners and hidden within the folds of the pleat. On especially long pieces of furniture, such as a daybed, extra seaming may be required along the length: these seams should be centred and the corner seams maintained. Alternatively, you may like to add a central pleat to accommodate this seam.

Gathered skirt

1 Begin by seaming pieces along the short edges to make a continuous length. First press the seam flat to sink the stitches, then press open. If needed, neaten raw edges using pinking shears, or zigzag stitch working close to the edge but not over it, to prevent fraying.

2 If the side edges form an opening, hem them as instructed for that particular type of closure.

3 Hem the lower edge by machine or, if you do not want the stitches to show through on the right side, slip stitch by hand. Working from right to left, pick up one or two main fabric threads and then slide the needle through the fold of the hem below, bringing it out about 6mm (¼in) along the fold. Continue in this way to complete the hem.

4 Set the stitch to 4mm (⅒in) and slightly loosen the upper tension. Work two rows of gathering stitches: one just above the seamline and the second 6mm (¼in) inside the seam allowance. Leave long thread ends. For gathering wide edges, interrupt the stitching at regular intervals or at intersecting seams.

5 Holding the bobbin threads, pull on them evenly until the gathered fabric fits the desired length. Fasten the ends around a pin and distribute the gathers evenly. Pin the layers together and tack close to the lower gathering stitches.

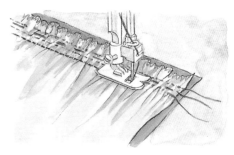

6 Using a normal stitch length and tension, stitch along the seamline with the gathered side upwards.

7 First press the seam flat, then press the seam allowance upwards.

Pleated skirts

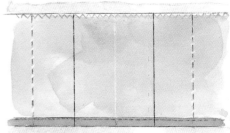

There are several kinds of pleat used on slipcover skirts: the most usual are the inverted, box and mock pleats. When constructing either inverted or box pleats, there are two lines which should be marked: the fold line, which is the edge of the pleat (right side) and the placement line, which is the line on which the fold is placed.

Unseamed inverted pleat

In this pleat, the folds are turned towards each other. On a tailored skirt, this type of pleat is positioned at corners, for example, on sofas and armchairs. Allow fabric for the finished skirt width, plus joining seams and twice the depth of each pleat.

1 Determine the depth of the pleat (ours is 10cm/4in). Mark the fabric on the wrong side with chalk.

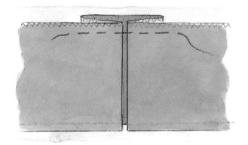

2 Place the folded fabric on the placement lines, press on both sides and tack across the top to secure.

Seamed inverted pleat

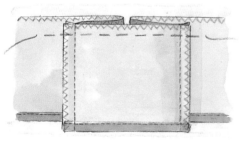

Add half the desired pleat width to each side measurement of the skirt length, plus seam allowances. Cut a separate underlay the full depth of the pleat, plus seam allowances. Join vertical seams and neaten the edges. Press. Fold and complete the pleat as for the single pleat.

Box pleats

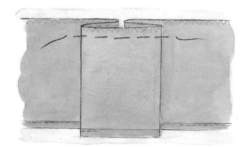

Here, the folds are turned away from each other. Box pleats may also be spaced apart but, in either position, the inner fold lines meet in the centre.

Continuous pleating

For continuous pleating, allow three times the finished skirt width, plus joining seam allowances. Place a pleat at each corner and at the centre front and back, then form pleats in between. Fold, press and tack across the top to secure.

Spaced box pleats

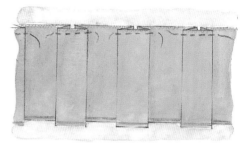

These pleats are usually spaced apart by the same measurement as the depth of the pleat. Mark the fabric on the wrong side, as shown, then fold, press and tack across the top, as for inverted pleats.

Mock pleats

As the name implies, these are not actual pleats but they give the impression that the fabric has been pleated. They are small rectangular pieces placed at corners behind the main fabric, where front and side skirts meet. Mock pleats are a simple and effective way to keep furniture feet hidden and give the cover a sophisticated look.

ESTIMATING SKIRTS

The two measurements necessary for calculating the amount of fabric needed are: the total skirt depth and the total skirt length. The depth is the finished measurement from floor to the skirt seamline (joining it to the cover), plus 1.5cm ($\frac{5}{8}$in) top seam allowance and hem allowance on the lower edge. The length (or width) is equal to the finished skirt top seamline, plus allowances for pleats or gathers, plus 1.5cm ($\frac{5}{8}$in) seam allowances for joining fabric widths and 3cm ($1\frac{1}{4}$in) for finishing ends.

WORKING WITH FABRIC

FABRIC FOR a loose cover should be closely woven and sufficiently heavy to hold its shape. Specially made furnishing fabrics are often treated to resist stains, creases and fading, making them practical and more durable than ordinary fabric, and should be chosen where possible. The width most commonly available is 122cm (48in) but selected fabrics in wider widths – 137cm (54in) and 152cm (60in) – are also available. The printed or woven design on a fabric is an important consideration and, before you buy, it is best to check your fabric choice for both colour and design. It is advisable to buy a large swatch and drape it over the furniture to be covered. Then, view it in different lights and from different positions.

Testing fabric

Before purchasing fabric, be sure that it is already pre-shrunk. If not, then it is advisable to pre-shrink a sample piece by machine washing or dry-cleaning, first making a note of its dimensions. Iron the wet fabric dry and and re-check the size. Allow for any discrepancy, adding the proportionate amount of the total length of fabric required.

Preparing fabric

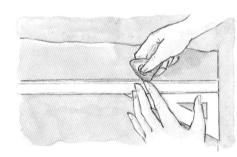

Before cutting out, prepare the fabric as follows: straighten the edge along the crosswise grain (where the fabric was cut from the roll). Placing a set square against the selvedge and a metre (yard) stick across the width, mark the edge with tailor's chalk, and cut across using sharp scissors or shears. Trim the selvedges to prevent the seams of the finished cover from puckering. Press if necessary.

Patterned fabric

If your fabric has large, dominant motifs in the design, you should plan how they fall within each section. On sofa and chair backs, they look best placed just above the centre, and on a cushion, in the centre. If you need to match motifs from one section to another, such as the two inside and front arms on a sofa cover, be sure to position them in exactly the same way on both sides. If you are cutting from a pattern, position identically if using on more than one piece. This needs to be considered in your cutting layouts but you should have already allowed more fabric for this purpose. (See also Ladder stitch for stripes and checks, pages 112–13.)

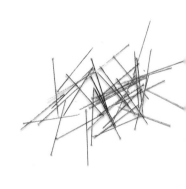

Transferring measurements

1 To do this, you will need a metre (yard) stick and tailor's chalk or marking pencil. Place the unfolded fabric on a flat work surface, right side up and, using the straight (crossgrain) edge of the fabric, measure off the distances as calculated for your cutting layout, lightly marking a few intermediate points along each line. Use the set square to ensure right angles where required. Mark all the sections in this way, double-checking against the measurements and grain lines on your cutting layout. If correct, go over the lines more firmly. If not, rub away the chalk line and re-mark the correct line.

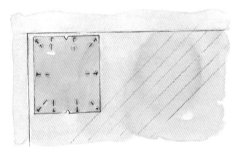

2 If you are using paper or cloth patterns, pin them to the fabric to secure. Make sure you position them on the lengthways grain; this runs parallel to the selvedges. Bias strips, however, are cut diagonally across the fabric, as indicated on the cutting layout.

Cutting out

Cut out the fabric sections with long-bladed shears. Transfer any construction marks and note annotations. You may wish to label the sections with letters, but for a beginner, it is a good idea to mark the name of each section on a piece of paper and pin it to the fabric. Lightly mark the lengthways grain and "Top" on the wrong side of each section. It is important to cut each piece on the exact straight grain and to stitch them together with the straight grain running in the same direction; this ensures that your cover will hang straight and "sit" well on the piece of furniture.

Pinking

This is a quick method of neatening fabrics that fray very little or not at all. The seam allowance is neatened after it has been pressed using pinking shears and cutting just inside the raw edge.

Making a paper pattern

In making a cover for an upright dining chair, for example, you may need to make a paper pattern for the seat shape, or back, depending on the style of the desired cover.

1 Using dressmaker's graph paper or ordinary wrapping paper, lay a sufficiently large piece of paper over the seat, so that it falls over the sides. Mark around the outside edge with a pencil, then cut into the back corners to allow for the chair back struts, if necessary. Mark the seam allowances and the straight grain arrows, running from north to south, and cut out the paper pattern.

Joining fabric widths

There are many instances in making loose covers where fabric widths need to be joined together. For example, on a long three-seater sofa, where the width of the fabric is narrower than the sofa. In such cases, fabric widths should be joined down the inside and outside back, the seat and border. On a sofa with two cushions, you may arrange to have a central seam aligned with the cushion joining – provided, of course, that two fabric widths would cover the areas mentioned.

1 As a rule, where two fabric widths need to be joined, one piece is cut in half lengthways and the two halves are then placed at either side of the full width. Where patterned or striped fabrics are used, match the pattern to the seamline – not the cutting line – and join the sections using the ladder stitch, see pages 112–13, before permanently stitching. Then, continue to fit and shape the sections.

Pressing

The technique for pressing involves placing the iron on the fabric with a pressing down and lifting up action, rather than sliding across the fabric. Careful 'pressing-as-you-sew' is the key to a professional-looking finish. Where possible, press on the wrong side of the fabric using a steam iron, or a dry iron with a damp cloth over the fabric.

Always press seams, tucks and pleats before joining intersecting seams. Press an open seam as follows:

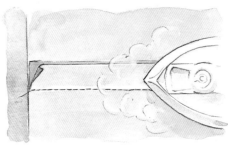

1 After stitching, finish off the thread ends and press the seam allowances to one side, to blend the stitches into the fabric.

2 Next, press the seam open using the point of the iron. Use the whole surface of the iron to finish pressing the seam allowance open. Neaten the raw edges as required.

Shaping to fit

Use the following techniques to control fullness at a curve, such as on the shoulders of a cover for a sofa or armchair or to allow for the width of struts on an upright chair.

Gathering

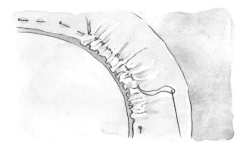

Pin both layers of fabric along the seamline up to the curved area. Then, using double thread, work running stitches by hand along the seamline edge to be gathered. Pull up the gathers carefully and evenly until the fabric fits the other edge, then secure the thread.

Tucks

Pin both fabric layers up to the curved area. Then, working outwards from the centre, form narrow equal folds along the longer fabric edge, until it fits the shorter edge. Pin and tack the tucks in place.

Darts

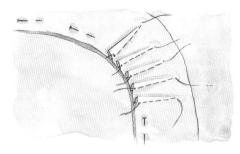

Pin fabric layers together up to the curved area. Then, working outwards from the centre, form narrow equal darts in the longer fabric edge to fit the shorter edge. Pin, tack and stitch the darts in place.

Mitre

To accommodate depth of furniture frames or padding, a mitre can be formed to shape a corner within a continuous piece of fabric. With the lengthways grain placed as shown, pin the fabric sections on both sides of the corner. Then pin the fabric along the corner. Trim the excess fabric to the seam allowance.

Wadding

Using wadding to pad the seats of chairs and sofas is optional, but it will make a hard surface softer and more comfortable to sit on. On furniture without upholstery, it is sandwiched between layers of the cover fabric but it can also be used as a smooth covering over buttoned upholstery beneath the cover. It should be cut into the appropriate pieces and simply laid on the upholstered sections, where it will stay put under the cover. It will cling naturally to the upholstery.

Use thick wadding for seat pads, making sure that edges are secured into at least one of the seam allowances. This will enable the pad to be cleaned without danger of the wadding moving out of place.

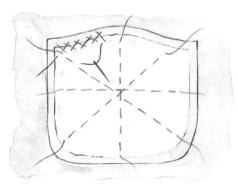

1 Using your chair seat paper pattern, cut out wadding to shape. Trim back the seam allowance. With one seat piece, wrong side up and the wadding on top, tack across both ways to hold the layers secure. Using the catch stitch (see pages 112–13), sew the edges of the wadding to the fabric seam allowance.

2 Place the second seat piece underneath, right sides together, and pin around the edge. Stitch around three sides, leaving the back edge open for turning through. Clip into the curved seam allowances, remove the tacking stitches, and turn through to the right side. Slip stitch closed, see pages 112–113.

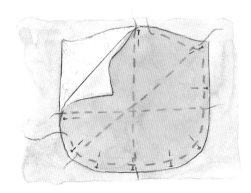

3 For a bound finish, cut out the fabric and wadding as before but do not trim the seam allowance on the wadding. Assemble the three layers: place the bottom fabric wrong side up, the wadding next, and the second piece of fabric on top, right side up. Tack across in both directions, smoothing the fabric and stitching outwards from the middle. Pin the edges and tack around just inside the seamline. Bind the edge as instructed in the project.

Lining fabric

Cotton sateen lining is widely available in a vast range of colours, furnishing widths and different qualities. It is commonly used for lining skirts of all types and, like other furnishing fabrics, it should be tested for shrinkage before cutting.

INDEX

ACKNOWLEDGEMENTS

picture credits

pages 7–15 Fabrics supplied by Anna French and Calico Corners

page 7 Adelphi Collection, Anna French

page 8 Tilbury Sandford Brysson Ltd (lace by Stiebel of Nottingham)

page 9 Avalon Collection, Anna French

page 10 Ballard Designs

page 12 *top left* Habitat UK Ltd; *top right* Mugshots/Ace Photo Agency

page 13 Habitat UK Ltd

page 14 Acacia Avenue Collection, Anna French

page 15 Ballard Designs

page 79 Tilbury Standford Brysson Ltd (sofabed by Deptich Designs Ltd, London)

supplier credits

page 35 Sofa, sofa fabric in Arles and cushions in Minara Check, all from Jane Churchill.

page 39 Ashleigh armchair and fabric in Hydrangea 82 from the Summertime Collection, backdrop fabric in Waterstripe FR 955 from the Acacia Avenue Collection, all from Anna French.

page 45 Sofa and fabric in Glenisla Check Taupe from Laura Ashley, cushions from Sanderson.

page 47 Chair fabric by Waverly in Classic Ticking Forest 605221, backdrop fabric in Angelica Meadow by P. Kaufman, both from Calico Corners; wrought iron pedestal with pointed glass bowl from Avant Garden.

page 49 Fabric by Sheila Coombes in Heversham H20 Radish, from Brian Yates Interiors.

page 53 Fabrics in Provence Stripe, Arles and Provence Check, all from Jane Churchill.

page 59 Edward chair from Ducal Ltd; Beaune fabric from Parkertex Proposals Collection; backdrop fabric by Sheila Coombes in Exotic Fruits 3669–01, from Brian Yates Interiors.

page 61 Edward chair from Ducal Ltd; Spring Posy fabric from Warner Fabrics; Petal Lace from Anna French.

page 63 Windsor chair from Ducal Ltd; fabric in High Days and Four Square from Sanderson; terracotta Provençal pot from Harwood Antiques.

page 65 Windsor chair from Ducal Ltd; Summer Glory fabric from Warner Fabrics; backdrop fabrics in Petal Lace and Romance Jacquard, both from Anna French.

page 67 Oakland fabric in Blue Colourways from Calico Corners.

page 69 Denim fabric from Calico Corners.

page 71 Chair from Mulberry, in St Ives Stripe GB004.

page 73 Chair from Mulberry, in Plain Natural Linen GB021.

page 75 Chair from Mulberry, in Navy Floral Rococo GB003.

page 81 Furniture from The Dormy House; fabric by Bloomcraft in Sea Island Sunshine, from Calico Corners.

page 83 Furniture from The Dormy House; fabric by Waverly in Cara Mia Fiesta, Cara Mia Stripe Fiesta and Florie Fiesta, from Calico Corners; backdrop fabric in Spinney Voile 3667–V1 by Sheila Coombes, from Brian Yates Interiors.

page 85 Furniture from The Dormy House; fabric by Waverly in Carabelle Rose, from Calico Corners; backdrop fabric Habotai silk 504D, from Pongees.

page 87 Futon from the Futon Company; fabric in Sundance Cactus and Hemingway Wine, from Calico Corners.

page 91 Furniture from The Dormy House; fabric in Crystal Natural from Calico Corners; backdrop fabric in Spinney Voile 3667–VI by Sheila Coombes, from Brian Yates Interiors.

page 93 Furniture from The Dormy House; fabric by Waverly in Stonington Wedgewood from Calico Corners.

page 95 Fabric from Calico Corners.

page 97 Fabric in Just Pink from Calico Corners; cake from Dunn's Bakery, London N8, UK.

page 99 Chair and fabric in Jacobean Linen FR 915 from the Summertime Collection, from Anna French.

pages 100–101 Over wicker chair, Côte d'Azur sheet from Collier Campbell; over wrought iron chair, voile fabric from Calico Corners; over padded stool, Waverley fabric in Cara Mia Fiesta and Florie Fiesta, from Calico Corners.

pages 102–103 Pine screen frame, slipper chair and footstool all from The Dormy House.

All silk flowers supplied by Judith Blacklock.

addresses

Laura Ashley
27 Bagley's Lane
London SW6 2AR, UK

Avant Garden
77 Ledbury Road
London W11 2AG, UK

Ballard Designs
1670 De Foor Avenue NW
Dept E4114
Atlanta, GA 30318–7528, USA

Judith Blacklock
PO Box 3219
London SW13 9XR, UK

Calico Corners
Walnut Business Park
203 Gale Lane,
Kennett Square, PA, USA

Jane Churchill
151 Sloane Street
London SW1X 9BX, UK

Collier Campbell Ltd
2 Clapham Common Northside
London SW4 0QW, UK

The Dormy House
Stirling Park
East Portway Industrial Estate
Andover, Hants SP10 3TZ, UK

Ducal Ltd
Andover, Hants SP10 5AZ, UK

Anna French Ltd
Head Office:
108 Shakespeare Road
London SE24 0QW, UK

Showroom:
343 Kings Road
London SW3 5ES, UK

Habitat UK Ltd
196 Tottenham Court Road
London W1, UK

Harwood Antiques
24 Lower Richmond Road
London SW15 1JP, UK

Mulberry Company Ltd
The Rookery, Chilcompton
Bath BA3 4EH, UK

Parkertex
PO Box 30, West End Road
High Wickham
Bucks HP11 2QD, UK

Pongees
Specialists in Silk
184–186 Old Street
London EC1V 9FR, UK

Arthur Sanderson
and Sons Ltd
6 Cavendish Square
London W1M 9HA, UK

Warner Fabrics plc
Bradbourne Drive
Tilbrook, Milton Keynes
Bucks MK7 8BE, UK

Brian Yates Interiors
Riverside Park, Caton Road
Lancaster LA1 3PE, UK